Eclectica Americana

Eclectica Americana

poems

E.M. Schorb

HILL HOUSE   NEW YORK

ISBN: 978-0-692-77548-6

Cover Painting "Big Red" by the Author.

Acknowledgements

Grateful acknowledgement is given the following publications in
which some of these poems, complete or in part, first appeared:
The American Scholar, The Antigonish Review (Canada), The
Antioch Review, The Arts Journal, Ascent, Atlanta Review, The
Beloit Poetry Journal, The Chariton Review, The Chattahoochee
Review, Chelsea, Chicago Review, The Cincinnati Review, The
Crab Orchard Review, The Deronda Review, Epos, Frank
(France), Ginosko Literary Journal, *The Great American Poetry
Show,* (anthology), The Haight Ashbury Literary Review, The
Hudson Review, *In Whatever Houses We May Visit* (anthology),
The Iowa Review, The Journal of New Jersey Poets, The Kansas
Quarterly, The Lake Superior Review, The Laurel Review,
Literal Latté, The Literary Review, The Massachusetts Review,
The Mississippi Review, Möbius, The New Welsh Review, N C
Arts, Nimrod, The Notre Dame Review, OffCourse Literary
Journal, Outposts (England), Poetry Daily, Poetry Salzburg
Review (Austria), Poetry Super Highway, The Princeton Arts
Review, Private Photo Review, Sand Literary Journal (Germany),
The Sewanee Review, Shenandoah, The South Carolina Review,
The Southern Humanities Review, The Southern Poetry Review,
Spring: The Journal of the E.E. Cummings Society, Stand
(England), Verse, The Virginia Quarterly Review, Voices Israel,
Wascana Review (Canada), The William and Mary Review, The
Wisconsin Review, The Writers' Forum, The Yale Review.

for Patricia

A fleece of fine doves
is too crude,
Patricia.

A fleece of fine doves,
murdered for love,
is not enough.

CONTENTS

PART ONE

THROUGH THE LOUPE

Great quiet things reside in viewpoint, if we think oddly enough. The leaf of grass, of course, when a child—how it looks to the ant like a frond. Life lied by size, pen lied by ink, later, everything lied, alas, and we grew up and filed it all away in Can't, or Won't, or in Beside-the-Point. We had a drink, and scratched our head, or ass, whichever itch went wild, because we were the parent now, and saw our children deride our uncertain augenblick with their sweet sass. Oh, we were foiled! But we toiled on. Our errands made us errant. We had failed, groom and bride, to remember the link between the parts and the mass, the link that was being spoiled— the lost current that powers the ride we take to the brink of life. Things pass, they pass quickly, as on oiled marble, in a torrent of time, while we in the loge pride ourselves, missing, like women in mink in the looking-glass, missing the opera, coiled, apparent, in the pearl.

NO ANGELS

I. SINGLEWIDE

If they thought of us,
how all of us lived in the singlewide, fourteen feet
deep and forty long,
on no money but the wealth of God
sending us on our mission,
bringing seven children, his, mine, and ours,
with the early death he bore in him, to leave
me, after five hard, bleeding years,
rooms spattered with blood, aplastic
anemia hemorrhages, him, my love, gone,
and me left with the beloved brats,
the marina rich would know
it was their Christian duty to buy us out
at a decent price.

I tell the buyers how God told us
this was where to stop,
how I planted the redtips to shade the
thin back from the sun, the fig from the Bible;
how I lost my faith in sorrow at his death
and drank my way
into Alcoholics
Anonymous and found
my new man there, who pumps iron,
sweats tea, but wants beer,
a tattoo'd boy not older, not
less wild, than my son,

and needing a mother-wife,
why we drink iced tea in winter in this cold
singlewide, how he hauls red-necked dynamite to
mines on eight fat wheels;
and the well-dressed buyers look at me
like I'm crazy as I tell them
I'll sell real cheap,
but not as cheap as the
marina rich will pay
for a sad eyesore;
and they don't think I know investors
when I see them, who'll put some other
poor souls in here, or tear it down for
the lake land; crazy because I will take
the money to Texas on the border to start my dream,
my homeless and battered women's mission.

My big lug's trucker's license goes far. Only
a relapse to fear, to drugs or drink,
can stop my heart's compassionate work,
or the mission is mine, to bring them the
visions of Isaiah and the trials of Job,
which I know in my used woman's body,
burnt-up with sex and sin, my pretty nose
and cheeks fried with small veins
from the days of bleeding and empty death.

The buyers smile in kindness at my dream,
my mission, my need for direction—
they think they are too smart and can
live without God. Well, let them, if they can.
How much will they give me for my life?   His anger

is not turned away and his hand is stretched out still.

I loved these woods that drop down to the rich man's
   lake,
condominiums, marinas, and the trees I planted to shade
my only wealth beside the Lord, my Savior.
But I bargain, with my stretch marks,
my unpainted, veined nose,
for my singlewide,
which no one wants, not even
these patient souls!

II. INCOGNITO

Le monde est le livre des femmes.
                              —Rousseau

Imagine arriving, ermine-clad,
thinking yourself forgotten there,
in a village in a valley, nearly a col,
ringed by alps, in one of those mysterious little
border countries in the Balkans, having chugged
uphill and tobogganed down until
you have left the other world behind,
where it is real and true, and have come finally
to your Ultima Thule, a guttural in a tongue
nobody outside knows; where,
stepping down from the powerful, steaming
train, containing the last of the known world,
you become again part of the place where you began,
unknown and young and beautiful and frightened,

decades and decades ago, before the shame and scorn.

Thanks to the enormous wealth you have amassed
as a world-famous courtesan, you have kept
your health and strength—money for monkey
glands, spas, etc.—and with them
some of the qualities you had
as a youth, particularly your fierce,
imperious temperament. And everyone moves at
the tilt of your wide-brimmed hat, everyone bows
—for even here there has been news of you—everyone
looks up at you in awe—your great height an
illusion created by power—and you say, finally,
after a lifetime of waiting: Bring them to me,
those who so hurt me that I had no choice but to
    succeed.

Your beautiful rival of youth waddles up.
She is just your age, but looks a thousand,
horrible, hairy. You sicken at the sight,
this porcine hirsute sight. She stole your man.
He stands beside her. What, not him! You give them
    alms.
But what of the dreadful mayor? Dead, long dead.
And what of your former employer, that hateful
    woman?
In a nursing home, gone daft with age. She sometimes
calls for you. They sweep you off to see her.
And she calls for you. You bring the bedpan in
yourself. You pat her hair. Where have you been,
you dreadful girl? You've been around the world
in company with kings. The *Almanach de Gotha*

mentions you. When your mistress falls into a
   comatose
dementia, a talking, tossing sleep, you watch the moon
sail across her curving window, and make a mental list.
Surely somewhere there is someone worthy of your
   wrath.

III. OLD WOMEN, PAUSING

Old women, pausing, standing midblock on a hill
or midlevel on subway steps, waiting for breath,
their shopping bags hanging from toughened hands,
their eyes back in girlhood, perhaps, or ahead,
on the next meal, the contents of the bags
cooked and served, their honor again earned,
exist away from where they are, the grade or incline
slowly flattening, reversing, as their hearts calm
and their breath comes slower, more peacefully;
and so they stand, with the stillness of statues,
black-coated, black-shod, eyes straight ahead,
wisps of pale hair riffling slightly with the breeze,
waiting for breath, ahead of or behind where they are.
—So all of us, ahead of or behind where we are
or separated from what we are, not complete,
having left part of ourselves behind,
not having done that which we hoped to do,
not having attained to that which we hoped to attain,
all like old women, standing midblock on a hill,
waiting for breath, ahead of or behind where we are.

IV. TRANSFORMATIONS

If in place of my lady's eyes
there were other eyes as beautiful,
if this woman had other eyes;

if my lady's eyes were emerald
like the Irish Isles and this woman's eyes
were violet like the flower;

if in place of my lady's hair
there was other hair as long and
wonderful to see and touch;

if this woman had different hair;
if my lady's hair was shot with gold and silver,
or gunmetal gray, and this woman's hair

was of that Oriental black, flashing green,
or rainbowed; if in place of my lady's ears,
other ears perched upon this woman's head;

if my lady's ears were curly, tiny cakes
with pink and white icing, cherried perhaps,
and this women's ears were brown and pendant,

with lobes like long strong loops, hung with spiral
shells;
if in place of my lady's upswept nose
there was the aquiline, or bulbous, or flat and flared;

if instead of my lady's pink aureoles

there were two burnished copper coins,
and if they made complete my lady's

perky breasts and the others did the same
for the pendulous breasts of the woman
by whom my lady was being replaced;

if my lady's slender waist vanished and became
another's,
girdled with lacy jeweled chains instead of Shantung
Pongee silk,
pale as Caucasian chalk or the limestone cliffs of Dover,

with belly button out instead of belly button in;
if my lady's pale round thighs, untouched by sun,
were found to be the lithe, athletic thighs

of a bronzed goddess who bathed all day in sun,
or thighs of Oriental gold or Melanotic mocha;
if my lady's ballerina's calves had been replaced

by hunger's calves in stockings made in diamond net;
if my lady's ankleted, once-bound feet, impossibly
small,
should be replaced by webbed paddle-feet, ruby-toed,

and dusted with reflective sand; and if my lady's
smiling mouth, containing pearly cubes in a row,
should be replaced by the bitter, appealing mouth

of someone else, another woman, with buff dentures
that had chewed raw meat, like a leopard's;

if, in short, my lady were replaced in her entirety,

and I beheld her there, upon that high pedestal
where I had placed her, should I approve?
If her soul could be the same, despite

the physical transformation; if she could say
the same words, the words that I had almost
come to understand, after ages of agonizing struggle,

I think that I should not know that she was a different
lady,
another woman, nor would it be true, in essence,
any more than I would be a different lover

without my beret, my bouquet of dew-damp,
fresh-cut, long-stemmed roses,
and my cornucopia of poetry.

V. NO ANGEL

for Patricia

Because you are you

& because they do not suffer
because their weather is never harsh
& they share nothing of the storms
that drive us in and burn us out
& because they are never in trouble
because they do not dance but on a pin

because they have no heat for anger
because they have no blood because
they do not eat drink nor defecate
& because they have no sense of humor
& because their lips are not discernable
but for a wide thin crease from ear to ear
& because their eyes are empty
but for the expansive light of heaven
& because they have not heard of sex
because they are never lonely
& because they do not judge
because they are not human
because they are abstract
& because their bodies are illusion
& because their wings beat nothing
& because they have no will but God's

you are higher than the angels

VI. THE NORTH OF LOVE

i.

Winter, that great doomed ermine,
challenges the serpent and the mouse,
buries each in his crude house,
silences the summer din
of birds: and bells ring across white silence
—where thickets are ungainly ghosts,
leaning together, gossiping in wind
—to herald a distant sleigh,

their chiming voices thinned
by the crystal distances of air
and the vast inertia of the trackless snow.

Through lacework windows
I see the bare white birch,
frail virgin of the timberline,
new bride of snow, the Eskimo;
I watch as he caresses
her modest, proffered limbs
and pale, gripping feet—
this mating of tree and snow
reminds me of all love . . .

ii.

When the phantasmagorial leafless trees blossom anew
    with blue, frozen tears,
and the wind-whipped snow at evening and the creeping
    mist make an indivisible ectoplasmic figure
that hovers above the lake and lurks near its frigid
    banks,
and the ominous cold evening sky describes the vale
    of lost things, with its gray upon gray of cloud
        upon sky,
and the moon is a pale disk in the pale, tall light
    of evening,
and the wind halloos down from the mountain like the
    voice of the Cyclops demanding more wine,

    and blindly it tumbles the house to one side;

when the dull, small stars go shivering about in the
    heavens,
and the serpent and mouse and the beaver and mole lay
    locked in their crude, white houses, afraid,

then we suffer from reminiscences of all the folly of
    the misspent years;
for winter is an end; above all a time of summing up:
    to take in hand and stop the spinning whirligig, your
life, to examine in the cold light how love fools,
    outflanks
you, takes you and makes you and breaks you again, no
    matter what sweet cynicism you think you have
        achieved. Do not try
to riddle this phenomenon any more than the heavening
hawk riddles his hunger. But remember the bare
    white birch, frail virgin of the timberline,

    the firnificated kisses of her bride-

groom gathering in cold, pallid clumps along her limbs,
    covens
of wind weighing against her, mountain-bred, bitter,
    flaying, as all love's too often made . . . .

iii.

I strengthen in this northern solitude:

When constellations wrangle overhead
and wind roars, the sudden shiftings cancel
the sound I listen for, the sound of bells,

and I fall into winter stupor, dreaming—
I dream of trekking up the mountainside,
the moon ahead, old-woman faced; behind,
the frail white birch, deflowered bride of snow.
I dream myself withstanding wind and cold;
and, breathing hard against the altitude,
of climbing up Love's Everest, to breathe
the cold significant wind of mountaintops.

VII. THE HONEY HOUSE

With its white picket fence and its little green lawn
and its rose bushes over here and over there in bud,
it was a picture book, a *Post* cover, a dream, of a house.

And it was theirs! But there *were* a lot of bees, weren't
     there?
It was the rose bushes, the wisteria, the dogwood, it was
the sweetness of their young love. She was pregnant—

bad to be stung by a bee she was trying to bat away,
     then
stung by another. She ran from the house and he came
     home.
Why, there was a beehive under the kitchen sink!

Then he saw that five bees had lit at the top of his paper,
which he shook, and he dodged but was stung just the
     same,
and the buzzing was deafening, he said, deafening.

So they called in the Masked Exterminator, who dis
    covered
that the house was filled with hives, ten feet tall in the
    walls,
right up through the floors. Didn't you see the honey?

Now in full summer the walls had begun to drip, the
    floors
oozed honey. Yours, said the Masked Exterminator, is
    a honeyhouse.
It's true, said the bride, I have washed it up and hosed it
    down.

And suddenly all were attacked and ran from the house.
Upshot: bride thought groom a fool and divorced him,
groom sued broker, who sought out former owner,

who had moved to Alaska, with intention of recouping,
supermarket tabloids did a number of stories on the
    house,
and, after her abortion, bride was invited to pose for
    Playboy.

PART TWO

THE RED SHIFT

When I angered you, you grew red in the face, and that red shift meant that you were leaving me, growing more distant, so I took your delicate hand and kissed it, uttering into it that I was sorry for any pain I had caused you, and the red faded from your cheeks, and gradually you turned pale with pink places, like an impressionist's dabs, here and there, neck and forehead, and I could see that the red shift was reversing and you were moving toward me again, the gravity of my larger body pulling you in like an angelfish on a fine silver line, like a seaward moon, like a meteor, and I thought what damage a meteor could do: a meteor could tilt me on my axis, could cause me to become engulfed in smoke, and blinded, and possibly extinct, so I pushed you back away from me. I held you at arm's length, and you began to turn red again, another red-shift, and that was not what I desired, so I pulled you to me and held you as tightly as I could, and, when I looked again, you had turned blue and your open mouth and eyes were dark, like holes in space.

AND/OR

I. PARTICLES
variations on a theme

/The Invocation

I lean forward
feel my body
but become
my mind
soul
doing bidding
informed
to do
each does
must do
be
tran
scribing
in gregg
pitman
keeping
track
keeping
up
with
dictator
fired
for art

listen
the poem
is on
the way
thank
AND the
bugles
blow
in the
OR world

/The Contemplation

AND
is making
what
AND knows
not OR

OR knows
what OR
makes
OR makes
what AND
knows

AND is
making

I make
this on a
field of
action
as I am
told by
my making
mind
AND's

can AND
make a
mistake
AND makes
everything
is OR's
best an
swer no
pangloss
served here
quack

/Quark

an
atom
charging
angrily

around
is never trying
to find a place
to light
for it
getting there
is all the fun
the relatives
will be boring
its friends forgotten
atom doesn't care
it's a dare
a dare
let me go there
AND there
AND there
more AND
more
AND
atom
get hotter AND
hotter
barely holding
its particles
together
looping around
its own light
around AND
around
pulling away
from the pull
of its own

gravity
elliptical
like a man
with a beer
belly
then
thin again
so fast
in such a hurry
to be
where
it's
in
scape
heartbeating out
ballooning
shaking
shining
shooting
rocketing off
OR
barking
wagging
hissing
OR
knifing up
green through soil
pressing
in in
visible
no-stas
is to

renaissance
budding
blooming
blossoming
bursting
blowing out
up away
AND
starting again
AND again
AND again
heart pounds
head thumps
brain
pulses
communicating
message received
before sent
it seems
ions
zip zap
where's
time
here
see the
labanotation
of bird feet
in mud they
dance now
still as
they fly
away

see /Envoi
the muddy
dance gert
see stein
sd
AND see prose
them flying is telling
being OR in poetry
AND naming
adamic
it is all on the field naming
I feel it a tree
the boy fielded the a snake
ball parvis
how he felt when it parvis
hit his glove
it was like light AND
like love help me
I am
like ein's but an
grace OR

II. NOTHING FOREVER

The end is where you start from.
—T.S. Eliot

Young fell forward
and the pistol fell from his hand.
He had been leaning on the stone wall of the bridge
and he toppled over
into the river, and was carried off to the sea.

23

Probably eaten.
For he never washed up.
The dark sky was huge
beyond humanity.
Young leaned against the moist stone wall.
The pistol
dangled from his left hand.
He looked and he saw
his own left hand with the pistol in it.
Now it was the hand of a murderer.
This had not been true,
the flick of a page back.
The flick of a page forward
and here he was—
a wave became a particle.
Someone thought him up.
Things must be observed to be.

Now you could see him
standing with the pistol in his hand.
Something thought the metal of the pistol up.
Something thought everything up,
observed it, and there it was,
like the river out there,
flowing under the stone bridge,
like the gleaming wet stones near the water.
He could see the lighted buildings
down near the bend of the river.
What dreams were being dreamed in them?
Where he was, it was too dark
for anyone in the buildings to see him,
but he was there, waiting to die,

neither dead nor alive, now falling forward.

Young felt an eerie déjà vu of being a child,
but with the gladness gone out of it.
It was the gladness that mattered.
Without it, nothing mattered.
These things were with him
as left the house with the mangled body in it
and made his way to the bridge,
this being a child but without
a child's joy.
Gladness, hope, optimism.
These were in solution in his fluids from birth.
Once, he would have loved this starry sky.
It would have led him to a grand future.
Young was thirty-five.
Nearly every morning of his life
he had seen a hopeful, open face in his mirror.
Now there was forever nothing.
Now even the stars did not know
of their own existence.
They had not yet formed senses,
nor, more, a mind.
They did not exist.
Nothing of the panorama of the night existed.
Nothing forever.

If eaten, he did not know it.
Did the fish taste him?
Why come to the bridge?
Why the pistol?
Well, he was a soldier.

The pistol was issued to him.
The bridge was somewhere between
France and Germany; Alsace, no longer existing.
But Young had been stationed there
for quite some time.
He was not an ordinary soldier.
He had been an investigator.
The Young who was no more had been
a policeman of sorts. The optimist.
The poet of gladness.
He had found an evil man.
Banal: it has been said since Hitler.

To Young the man's cause was small.
Look at the size of the sky!
A little political cause, temporal merely,
for which the man had killed many people.
Bombs on innocent heads, exploding letters
in innocent hands. It made Young sick.
Isn't there a way of understanding these things?
What are small, evil things, anyway?

Do they occur because we observe them?
ORs, part of the great AND.
Everything is explained then, in the AND.
The AND is the end and the all,
a sort of heaven with explanations.
Young had comforted himself
in this way for years.
ORs and the AND.
It was a way of explaining
the ugly parts of life,

the big fish eating the little fish,
the fact that he had become a soldier,
and then a very special kind of soldier,
the kind who dresses in mufti, carries
secret weapons on his person,
the kind who lies about what he is.

At twelve, thirteen, fourteen, fifteen. . .
he began to wonder back.
Somewhere in there he began to wonder
back to the sky, to the sky's beginning.
Spring and green grass and flowers again.
He lay on his back in a field and studied the sky.
Graffiti said God was dead.
But what was this then?
The chemistry of his optimism
could not accept graffiti's dictum.
Something meant all this.
But why would life be made like this,
with everything eating everything else?
It was horrible.
In school they fed insects to the frogs.
In National Geographic
people ate one another—long pig.
What kind of being would have made this?
An evil one? It shocked his young soul.
He looked at the grass and then
at his hands. Fine hairs were beginning to show
on the backs of his hands.
But it was a beautiful spring day.
New flowers everywhere.
The ground was soft from an early rain.

The grass cushiony. The sky blue.
White clouds. Faces? Things?
ORs. ORs in the AND.
Not God but AND.
No need to know now.
Know in the AND.
Then everything will be resolved.
Goodness will answer any question.

Later, it was not hard to be a soldier.
Soldiers were ORs.
War was an OR, not an AND.
Young concerned himself with the OR-world.
Someday his questions, his doubts,
would be answered. Now, he functioned
without doubts.
They were for later,
and then to be resolved.

He attended West Point,
liked mathematics,
became an engineer.
He wanted to build things—bridges.
He liked bridges. He wanted to build
bridges between people too.
He wanted the world of people
connected by bridges of good faith,
truth, honesty, love.
Soldiers had become peace-makers
and peace-keepers. Peace is our Profession,
it said on the side of SAC bombers.
After the examination for West Point

he did very well indeed.
He was very intelligent,
not without an active imagination.
Bridges between stars.
They must be very flexible, yes,
he agreed with a fellow cadet
who had laughed at his good-natured fancy.
All bridges should be flexible.
Stress and strain. Sturm und Drang.
Trees bend with the wind and do not break.

Where was the stone bridge that he came to then?
It had not been observed by him as yet—
it did not exist.
But in its non-existent state
two armies clashed for its possession.
It had been strafed, bombed, and strafed.
Displaced Europeans had jumped from it,
into the river where he was going,
even then, before the bridge existed.
The bridge was an OR and
appeared to him only on the night of his death,
when he wandered to it,
wounded, bleeding, and seeking a way out.
Others who had crossed it or
gone under it had never seen it before.
Rats lived near it, Young had noticed.
Once, people hid under it,
from the bombers, the strafers.
Once, people lived under it,
from the dislocation.
It had appeared to all of them

for the first time once, even its builders,
appeared out of nowhere in a century
that no longer exists,
was observed by someone, somehow,
somewhere, even before it was there.
On paper, presumably,
only the history of the hand drawing it,
mort main of time.

Young loved order.
The military suited him in this.
Life on the parade field.
Nothing so aimless now
as that spring day way back
when he was child, a growing boy.
Now he liked everything to have a point,
a purpose. Time and motion.
Young played soldier with his brother.
They marched with broomsticks
on their shoulders. They copied the movies.
Left flank, right flank, ho! It was fun.
In one movie, a favorite of the brothers,
there was a battle over a bridge.
Two armies clashed.
Planes dropped bombs and strafed.
It was very exciting.
Young and his brother built
the little bridge in the park
near their home out of bits of wood and pebbles.
They made it span a tiny rivulet
of rain-water from a puddle, and,
late in the afternoon, when it was time

to go home, they dropped rocks on it
and smashed it down. The bridge in the movie
was in another world. Older men, uncles,
big brothers, went to it and came home,
or didn't come home.
Stars were hung in windows.
You could see them all over town.
Then, soon, they knew where the places were.
They kept track.
Young was growing up.
He would become a soldier.

But he would never meet
an implacable evil, no,
and he would never kill
such an evil in cold blood.
No, not like the different fishes,
stonefish, sharks.
No, he would never
torture a man with many wounding shots,
never make the man beg to die.
Only the enemy did that.
You saw it in the movies.
He would never torture a man
into admitting his evil.

"Say how empty you are! Tell
how you have wasted your own life
along with the lives of others!"
That would be taken care of in AND.
Young could not imagine hating anyone
so much that the gladness of his chemistry

could turn into a toxic grief.
Young could not imagine being sick
to his cells with hatred.

Young saw the sky one spring day or other.
Young suckled warm milk
from his mother's breast and learned love.
Young was conceived in love,
a twinkle in the eye of eternity.

III. PEACE IN OUR TIME

O yet we trust that somehow good
Will be the final goal of ill . . .
—Tennyson

The poet, ignorant philosopher,
Alpha & Omega beggar, posits
AND, in an academic naming, the
world that takes all others in:

"AND," he says, "includes the All.
OR is us & even war.
AND will keep including more.
OR is reductive, what we recall

—particulars, parts, & particles
—how many ways can it be said?—
all things unborn, & all things dead,
commas, grapes, seeds, articles

of various sorts, & written ones,
all things that are not All,
all memories we can recall,
all less than All, all suns,

all galaxies, germs, & viruses,
all parts of atoms & their parts,
all stops, reverses, starts,
all flowers, roses, irises—"

She frowned. "And so you say," she said,
"that you can live with ugly war
because it's what you call an OR.
ORs also are the many dead!"

"Yes. When struck by this, I wondered
what horrid meaning it must have.
The morality of love
was made to seem almost a blunder.

And yet, I thought, morality
must include the act of war.
For Fascists must be fought, are OR,
are fragments of eternity

gone wrong in AND, the All; are Fear.
A kinder & a gentler love
has got to be beyond, above,
& other than, this OR-world, where

it must be that, if we could see
the whole of things, we'd understand

how piece by piece (& hand in hand)
things add to form in synergy

a greater than is each alone,
as also are twinned Space & Time,
or life in clay & death in lime.
Thus, in the AND, all Ors atone."

WATERFALL

for Ed Bosch

Reflected mountains
bushes trees and below
crazily slanting vistas
gems half buried
in landscapes
as if the flow
had discovered
a sunken treasure
unmanufactured
axes arrowheads
raw material
of a stone culture
and casting over all
over reflected
layered escarpments
tiny rock flowers
bits of blue
scarlet and gold
reflected skies

full of mysterious
darting shadows
unseen birds
swaying branches
wind-caught leaves
and wading a long bend
found Ed on a great
rock arms akimbo
chest heaving
then pointing up
through thick trees
and followed his gaze
seeing deeply hidden
in brush bramble
tangle a small cabin
grayed by weather
Ed called "Poet!"
Wading on waist-
deep we came to
our umpteenth
small waterfall
and had to climb
our way around it
up a steep embankment
of black mud and green moss
fingers and feet
ripping upheaving
fine smooth moss
scurrying afraid
of a long
uncontrollable slide
backwards

onto jutting rocks
and then at last
able to drop down
into cool water
mud washing from feet
dipping hands
in purling water
and washing mud
from knees
water here only
four or five
inches deep
but stepping into it
surprised by its
force pressure
for an instant
thinking it
might topple me
but learning
one must flow
not fight the stone
underfoot
put down a foot
with all its
muscles loose
let it find
its shape on the earth
looked up
saw an
overawing
escarpment
circling in deep

beautiful
rainbow folds:
hitting an odd rock
the waterfall fell
out like an opening fan
or like two falls
translucent lovers
entwined and
undulating
and above them
below the deep
blue heaven
a cliff hung
weighted with trees
I knew a magic place
when I saw one
and vision
an Oneida chief
stood on the cliff
smiling
in full regalia

PART THREE

WINGS

Generally, children are not allowed to get tattoos, so the boy had wings drawn on his back with a marking pencil by his friend. He had a long, narrow back, relatively speaking, so the wings had to be long and narrow, from his shoulder blades to his behind, where the pointed tips disappeared into his yanked-up short pants and came out behind his thighs. His friend objected that the pants would prevent the wings from opening, so, after a few moments of thought, the boy dropped off his pants and stood naked at the edge of the cliff. "How do you know this is going to work?" asked his friend. "It is going to work because these are not the wings of a bird," said the boy, "but of an angel." And he jumped and swooped down over the water and then swooped up again and flew into the clouds. "Goodbye," called his friend, the artist, and "Goodbye" called the angel, waving.

ALL SOULS

I. THE LOSS

When the blackbird stood on the chimney and called,
poking her beak at the clear blue ice of the sky,
I watched from inside the frame of an old wooden house
across from the once two-chimneyed house where she
   stood,
heard her cry crack the ice of the sky that day
from the wrongest of chimneys, the wrongest.
The bricks lay scattered next to the house.
The big nest of hay had blown away.
The ugly babies now lived in the barn,
but for one, who had drowned in the well.

II. ELEGY

This compass-headed bird,
                dead-reckoning South in Fall,
arcing its bloody breast
                above the roof and cawing
some kind of bold farewell
                to higher air and leaderless
V'd fliers off on it,
                was shot (we saw and heard),
and staggered in the sky,
                dripping blood and guts
down on the lobstered roofers
                working in the sun.

It sang its downfall swan
                 song silently, now, spread
its wings, and then, as silent
                 as its eyes, it lay
resting on the roof,
                 face up, and looked at clouds,
(and some sweet heaven we
                 could almost see); but soon
pain shook it like an angry
                 nurse, so one good roofer
struck head from body with
                 a spade, merciful severance,
and catwalked off, bloody
                 spade dragging on the tiles,
a man of dirty duty,
                 unlike the murderer
of song, the wanton boy-
                 in-man, who pellet-shot
the bird (the shot we heard);
                 and this once musical,
most bright and beautiful,
                 small dust was part of all.

III. THE SOULS

Outside on a green lawn a giant water-oak conducts a
    sunset.
    Some unsteady hum has summoned us out of our
       houses.
My ancient lady friend, who lives nearby, is jawing
    now, and wears

an awed-holy expression as she says they are souls,
yes sir.
And they are everywhere, they wade the dusky clouds,
they are
giant black-winged fruits hanging, falling, bouncing.
The green
is black with them. And neighbors stare; they worry for
their

cars and pickups. If they get into the red berries, it's
hell on
paint. Shoot them. No, they are beautiful. They are a
menace.
Look out below! They rise and wheel, kaleidoscopic,
inside rings
of themselves. They set themselves against the sky,
black on blue.
They caw. They are telling themselves, or us, some-
thing.
They caw and caw, and what is it they are saying, so
earpiercingly, holes through your eardrums, through
your brain,

as if lasered? Then they settle again, like a black
blizzard
of huge coal flakes. The souls come back to visit us,
to tell
us that they know everything now. Now their sharp
yellow beaks
pierce the lawn. They are busier than worms, in a
feast
of famishment, an ecstasy of appetite. Now, she says,

the nonagenarian, I'll soon be with them, and then
it's always now for me like them. The souls have found
their

bodies. I don't know which is which, but somewhere,
there,
is everyone who died, all the loved ones, and even the
others,
the ones that nobody loved, they are all there now, she
says.
I stare as deep as I can see. They are every blessed
place—on roofs, looking down, in trees, on bushes,
under,
over, and around. Some seem to be waiting, some tug
at the turning-emerald lawn in the lowering light: and
now

how do they know to rise suddenly, and become one
wide
black wing? How do they know to circle and circle in
unison,
one boomerang black wing composed of so many
blood-beating,
sky-rowing black wings? How do they know when
it's time
to fly along a horizon, rimmed with rising red? The
souls,
they know, they know! I think it must be out of some
distant
folklore that the old lady speaks, eyes fixed, waving
them goodbye.

IV. TO A RAT

Rat, you frighten me,
though I understand perfectly well
that I as well frighten,
indeed frightened you,
coming around the corner
from the garbage bag,
your whiskers winking
on your corrugated snout
and your two little
beads of eyes glinting,
black beads
with some little mind
behind them
and a soul.

Ah yes, you have a soul:
I saw it with my own two
frightened eyes,
little rat.

I was alone
when you waddled
around the corner,
saw me and, for an instant,
flattened everything about yourself,
sniffing snout,
bead eyes,
long gray tail,
then scampered off,
terrified,

like the rat that you are,
you rat,
you dirty rat,
you poor little devil,
you sad little pilferer,
you filth, you pest,
you spreader of plague,
you biter of babies,
you rodent,
you cousin
of the bright-eyed squirrel,
you poor
relation, you scum,
you inelegant bum!

Now there's a trap
in the corner
with a cheese slice in it.
Don't make it snap.
Things are tough
enough
as they are.

PART FOUR

HUMANS, PEACE, AND THE RUMOR OF WAR

There is no war! Not over here, not over there, nowhere, in fact. There is no war and now we must ask ourselves the following questions: Whence come our new inventions? How are we to learn to pack food? Will the population explode? Will the over-taxed planet wither? And just as the questions were becoming hysterical cries, the old boom began again, on the far side of the quiet mountain, and the relieved people began to stand tall and sing their great songs of defiance, as if there had never been a moment of peace.

TATANKA IYOTANKA

Double Ballad Of Sitting Bull

Sioux must have mounts. Sun-Dreamer,
        greatest of all shaman,
        advised, Go
        to the horse-rich Crow.
        Up from Mexico,
    stolen by Comanche,
    passed north to Utes, Shoshoni,
    the best mounts came, finally,
        to the Crow.
So a hundred Hunkpapa
went on the warpath, the
        Sioux seeking Crow
in Yellowstone summer,
    lariats ready, led by Sitting Bull,
        finding and making off with many a Crow
    pony.

From French frontiersmen—coup, to touch or to strike
    the enemy.
    Let aftercomers slay
    him: you are first in honor because first in the
    fray.
Slow, who,
    at fourteen, had no other name—he
was considered deliberate, thoughtful,
    not slow—must join the hunting party—
        but out on the trail,
    so his mother could not try to stop him,

would not hold him back and
wail
    as if he were riding to his death. Deliberately,
Slow must be fast, first, must make coup

    Pursued! so that along the
                  skyline the rays of rising sun
                  were
            made of long wide rare
            red feathers, each on a spear.
      Crow galloped—Sioux galloped.
      Now Sioux must be intrepid—
must hold the herd! Winter Rides,
            the Crow Chief,
sent Sitting Bull a challenge
to a duel on the range,
            just chief and chief
in single combat. They
   knelt, aimed, and fired. Sioux and Crow
   prayed. Both sides
   waited for the white cloud to clear. Winter
   Rides was dead,

or die now and be done, for "It is better to lie naked
   than to rot on a high
   scaffold," an old man who has lived safely, afraid
   to die,
now naught
   but bent bone and thin loose flesh for the
sun to cook and the crows to eat. A name
   must be earned. Let the braves mock his war
               lust—who cared?—but he

would have greatness, and he must begin.
He will not allow anyone in
the
world to stop him, not mother nor sisters nor
mocking braves
nor even father. And so he caught

Sitting Bull's round shield pierced, the
           sole of his foot penetrated and
           badly mangled, and
           his legendary limp
     acquired for American
     history. And now a grand
   chief, famous, mighty, un-
           defeated,
with his every step, he
reminds all who see
           how he can spread
over the prairie the
     Sioux's high might and exclusive
     dominion,
   for there were fewer and fewer bison.
     These hunting grounds,

and joined his father's band, saying, of himself and his
pony,
*   "We are brave and strong, and*
*   are going too." On his father's face he saw*
*   pride, and*
"A brave
*   is a brave when he proves it," and Slow*
had already killed his first buffalo;

had touched a dead foe's face. He gave Slow
his own coup-stick, then
prayed to the Great Bull Buffalo God
to keep Slow safe in the
band—
for who would forgive him Slow's death?—then
willed that Slow be
first to send an enemy to his grave.

which had once belonged to the
Crows, Hidastas, Rees, Shoshonis,
and
poor, dying Mandans,
once many and grand,
could not keep such numbers.
The Treaty of Fort Laram
-ie, which held the tribes to peace,
Sitting Bull
declared, must be broken or
his people starve, and by
1864,
all the chiefs who had signed
the Treaty of Fort Laramie with the
Sioux nation were dead, their tribes driven
off and hiding,

Then it was hard riding, to where the bubbling, blood
red water
of the Missouri river
turned brown, and there were the Iroquois, taking
from the giver,
brothers

to vultures, stealing their bison—meat,
hoof, and hide—from the hungry Hunkpapa,
who would ambush the Iroquois but
       for the gold-painted
     boy, crying, "I am Slow, bravest of the
          Hunkpapa," who charged
         ahead
of his band to make coup on an isolated Iroquois
hunter, alarming the others.

    afraid to hunt buffalo
          at all, Sitting Bull having
          triumphed.
        "Chief Sitting Bull fed
        the nation," Sioux said,
     "on thirty-five thousand
bison a year." "Grandfather,
my children are hungry," prayed
        Sitting Bull,
when taking aim at a great
bull buffalo, "so I
         must kill you. It
is what you were made for."
    Then he offered meat to Wakan Tanka,
        Double-of-the-Sun, who had given bison
        their meat.

Now the surprised Iroquois hunters turned in retreat—
   all but
     one brave, who stopped, turned about,
     and drew his bowstring. But coup! Slow struck
     him with a shout,
and fame

was Slow's, as other Hunkpapa slew
the unfortunate brave. Sitting Bull, Slow's
great father, felt his pride overfull

as the others circled
his son Slow with raised weapons in salute
of his courage in battle.

He must give some away. He, Returns-Again,
now Sitting Bull,
awarded Slow his honored name.

THE WHITE STALLION

It seems there is a place
where beggars and poor people go to tell tales,
and the mostly riding moon will park to look
and to listen in the dark to the tales as they are told
    by the poor beggar bards of the hobo jungle,

    a place lonely as life,
at the end of the track, in a cul-de-sac
of starred, campfired night, in a turntabled copse
in the dark ragged green of smoke-stunted oak and
    rope-strong
        weeds, where birds bivouac: and of all beggar
        bards

        who sang a sad ballad
there, for the folk, or chanted a moon-watched tale,
the most famous because most magical was
the hobo bard the Pinkertons called "The All-Seeing
    Eye,"

because of his blind, superhuman vigilance,

and the mooncalf folk called
"O'Shay the Irish Shaman" for his gift of
curative power, uncanny control
of events, and for divining the deep, hooded meaning
   of things beyond their poor eyes and plain powers
   to see.

Now O'Shay rose up and
loomed before them, above them, his flame-mapped
   face
red and changing as the cat-o'-nine-tailed fire,
his great, blind eyes like those of the horse of his inner-
   eye
   (a carp-eyed stallion), his hair a red, swimming
   flame

dowsed by the cool waters
of the moon. O'Shay, though blind, was free, though
   poor,
was proud, and did not like to see the poor folk
bowed by that boulder, Care, nor bullied by the railroad
   dicks
   and afraid in their camp at the end of the track

underneath the parked moon
in the starred, turntabled copse where he loomed now,
watching their weak eyes with his strong, inner one,
and knowing that they needed a hopeful tale to be told
   that the Depression be lifted, courage restored,

and the parked moon set free
to ride the night into dawn, and new hope for them,
crying: "Pride's the subject of my moon-watched tale.
Now listen to O'Shay, poor people, and see what you
    think
        stop, look, and listen with the fascinated moon.

"There was a white stallion
that lived when you were but babes of scuttlebutt
at heaven's height; nay, that moon itself unborn
of the great, swaying sea; a stallion of clouds and spirit
        that came finally to gallop the great plains of

"the North American
west; a pale, proud, bellows-nostrilled, carp-eyed king
of a horse, that could blow back the floozy wind
from Manitoba down to the plains of old Mexico;
        that could whinney across the west to call a brood

"mare from her happy home
to him a thousand miles away in the night;
that spoke in trumpeting tongues of his freedom,
stamped, and neighed pride from his great, rampant
    heart; who hammered hope
        with his hooves to the ranging mustangs of the
        plain.

"A maverick king, he!
And this is the best part, for the horse was blind
like myself, and nothing daunted, unconstrained,
for he saw with his four, steamed, cow-catcher hooves,
    and his ears

that could hear the baby-breath sigh of a willow

"on an unborn wind; saw,
too, and best, with an inner eye like my own,
and had powers, like myself, gifts of nature,
with which he could divine the treachery of humankind,
    and thus keep himself free, and wear no man's
    hot brand.

"For he wore no man's brand;
and that was a heartache to all rich ranchers
who had heard of the white stallion: his freedom
mocked their staked, barbed wire; and they offered gold
    for his capture—
        pots of rainbow gold those rich ranchers offered
        the

"buck who captured the horse;
gold, gold beyond a poor cowpoke's wildest dreams—
fifty thousand dollars in gold bullion to
the buckaroo who brought in the phantom of the
    prairies,
        fifty more to the bronco buster who broke him—

"fifty thousand in gold,
one hundred thousand in gold bars to do both!
They came from the stretched limbs of the continent—
wranglers, roustabouts, beggars and poor people like
    ourselves,
        all with mad schemes to capture the blind, white
        stallion,

"keen on the trace of gold."
Here O'Shay's brick jaws mortised, his lips ringed
    teeth,
and his dark sockets fixed face after face, saw!
And yet they knew O'Shay was a blind man and could
    not see
        the mad excitement that they felt, hearing of gold,

        could not see how they stood
who had sprawled or hunkered down on their heels
    here,
could not know, therefore, how ready for pursuit
they were, how each in his mind saw a fleece-white
    phantom flee
        his grasp, as O'Shay took pause from his moon-
            watched tale,

        and they cried out to him
suddenly, as one many-voiced, to go on.
"Mad men with mad schemes!" cried O'Shay. "For
    they knew,
the earthly fame of the phantom being, by now, wide-
    spread,
        that all the ordinary methods of capture

        "had been tried and had failed.
No, a ghost must be caught in some other way.
Hence these mad or tragic traps. One loon dreamed of
speeding hoopsnakes that would ensnarl the steed's
    cow-catcher hooves,
        another's gold-frenzy fancied a fast balloon.

"The supernatural
horse and the idea of gold had made them mad.
Not all, some had sounder brains and better schemes.
A wrangler, a strong man who knew his horses, had
    staked out
    an arroyo which was the haunt of the white steed.

"He pitched camp and waited;
and happenstance his patience was rewarded
when, like a mirage, the pale, maverick king,
with his own remuda of mares prancing and curvetting
    behind, galloped up to drink, stamping and
    snorting.

"The wrangler climbed a rise,
and, twirling an Indian-charmed lariat
of rawhide interwoven with shot-gold wire
which he had bought from a Kiowa shaman, roped him,
    looping the golden noose neatly around his neck.

"The white stallion whinnied,
rose rampant, and snapped the charmed, magic lasso
as the wrangler might have snapped a golden thread;
and the still-noosed stallion and his mares vanished in
    white dust.
    But this was the closest that any man had come."

O'Shay stopped his story
here, drank from his flask, wiped his mouth up his
    sleeve,
and looked intently out at the poor people,
who had begun to suspect that he was not blind at all,

58

so seeing seemed his ragged, flame-valanced
   sockets.

      And now they felt that he
could see them fingering their necks, golden-noosed
now, like that of the horse of his long, tall tale;
fingering their necks and feeling the golden noose
   tighten
      as they pulled from the shaman, and snap, free-
      ing them.

      Suddenly O'Shay laughed,
and the rubbernecking, neckrubbing folk shook:
but then there seemed to have been no laughter there
but merely the bark of dogwood flame from the heeling
   fire
      or the sudden gold caw of a blackbird, bivouacked

      nearby. O'Shay frowned, now
and said: "Having heard how the wrangler had failed,
the rich ranchers upped the purse to a million;
but before any could claim it, he must represent them,
      having won a competition for horsemanship

      "from among the finest
cowhands and vaqueros to be found; and then,
having conquered all men, must conquer the horse.
The competition involved every truck or skill of
      wrangling science and art, and lasted a twelve-
      month.

      "A vaquero triumphed,

and had fine mounts stationed at mile intervals
from a wheel's hub out for a hundred hot miles,
the hub the arroyo where the horse had escaped the
    noose,
        the fine mounts the posed spokes of a great
        wagon wheel.

        "The vaquero waited
at the hub of the wheel for the phantom horse
until it appeared, and the pursuit was on
for a hundred miles, mile on hot mile, with fresh, mile–
    new mounts,
        for the vaquero hoped to exhaust the phantom.

        "But the great vaquero
could not exhaust or overtake the white steed,
who taunted him with his easygoing gait;
and, after his hundredth horse had dropped, could only
    report
        that the golden noose still hung from the phan-
        tom's neck.

        "News of the hunt's failure
spread up and down the plains, told by range riders
on lonely duty tours, at starred, campfired night,
until word reached a famed trapper up in Manitoba,
            one who had trapped every kind of animal.

        "His name was Hawkeye Red."
O'Shay paused here to take a swig from his flask and
to consider the beggars and poor people,
who were amused by the blarney of their shamrock
    shaman,

who again managed to relate himself to

the pacing white stallion.
A few friendly hoots were heard, with which, O'Shay,
scrunching a flame-snake of brow in a dark wink,
returned to his tall, romantic tale. "Hawkeye Red," he
    said,
        "left his cold northern home and journeyed far
        southwest

        "to find the white phantom,
or to find out where he might be found. Then he
methodically began work on his great trap.
He gathered the strongest oaken lumber that could be
    found
        and built a great stable in the arroyo where

        "the horse was golden-noosed,
and in it placed the most beautiful young mare
that the rich ranchers possessed among them, a
doe-eyed, blazed-faced bay with black mane and tail.
    Ringbolt-tethered,
        high-strung, frightened, Bonny-Pru would be the
        bait.

        "Now he set the trap doors,
cleverly contrived to clap shut behind the
white horse when, or if, he entered, trapping him.
After making sure that the trap would work, Hawkeye
        Red and the rich ranchers went to a vantage point

        "to wait for the phantom.

Under the riding moon, Bonny-Pru pulled, kicked
the oaken planks, and whinnied for her freedom
across the dappled night, until her fearful, fearsome
    cries
        were borne as on an unborn wind to the white
        steed.

        "The man-watched moon rode high
as the hours passed and nearer and nearer he
galloped with all his magical might toward
her in her trap, and his; but at last he came to the dark
    and looming stable; and, though the great, mouth-
    ing doors

        "gaped open, paused, galloped
away, circling wide the foreboding building;
then, though he knew this was a trap, galloped in
to the distressed, stable-trapped, ringbolt-tethered
    damsel mare
        who cried out for a brave champion like himself.

        "The trap doors shut! Silence.
No sound whatever from inside the stable.
The rich ranchers whooped high for their victory;
but, somehow, Hawkeye Red, now rich, felt saddened
    by success.
        All left their vantage point and approached the
        stable.

        "But, nearing it, the doors
split, splintered like kicked glass, spilled, filled the
    spiked air,

and up and over the heads of Hawkeye Red
and the rich ranchers rose the white steed and his
    damsel mare
        like two wide-winged, magical, legendary birds.

    "Hawkeye Red shook his head
in unbelief, turned, dazed, to see them, bullets
that followed the riflings of infinity.
In a moment of wild, unholy desperation, he
        ran to his horse, reached for his rifle, aimed and
            fired.

    "The rifle exploded,
but from the breech, not the muzzle, blinding him.
And in that first blind instant he saw the horse
of his mad pride go free, the white phantom rise ram-
    pant and neigh,
        like a musical muscle that flexes and sings,

        "and vanish from the land,
with his blazed-faced bride, Bonny-Pru, by his side,
never to return again." The poor people
were on their feet, now, whinnying, and galloping in
    place,
        for O'Shay had turned them into happy horses

        who would wear no man's brand,
who applauded their pleasure with hoof-clap hands
and tongues that rode the roofs of moon-watched
    mouths.
"Hawkeye Red," he said, "regained his vision, but saw
    no more

with his outer eyes but with a strong, inner one,

"and lived to tell the tale
at the end of a track, in a cul-de-sac
of starred, campfired night, in a turntabled copse
in the dark, ragged green of smoke-stunted oak and
rope-strong
    weeds, where birds bivouac." And he set the
    moon free.

COPPERHEADS

The New York Draft Riots

Vanish these walls, vanish this wealth, with visionary
    eyes that see
back to hot July 1863. Vanish where wealth shines
    shopping on Fifth
Avenue, five minutes from the lion-braced library,
    where I turn down
my book. Vanish these great, gray walls, to see when
    this mirage
was another, of a white-winged building housing
    motherless humanity.
Try to see out of the eyes of two hundred frightened
    black orphans

and their saviors, or, better, the eyes of one little girl
    under her bed,
who is to be beaten to sleep and burned alive. They
    come now, the first,

malignant rumble of mobs is heard. A giant, bearing a
    huge American flag,
appears. Ten thousand men and women follow. They
    shout: *NO DRAFT*;
shout: *KILL THE NIGGERS*! One mob of ten thousand,
    among many mobs,
one mad mob, is coming; Copperheads coming; but
    Mary doesn't know

what they are. Snakes, she is told; and, people like
    snakes. Snakes?
What does it mean?   But behind them the sky is red, as
    if the sun had
set in broad day, as if it had hit the earth and bounced
    back to the sky
in cones of flame, like upward teeth, serrating the
    downward, hot blue.
The fireworks for the Fourth, a week before, had shaken
    her.
Looking everywhere, she saw no arms to hold her.
    BOOM BOOM!

Now again—*BOOM BOOM!* But this is wilder, worse.
    She caps her ears,
her eyes rolling for a mother, while the giant bearing
    Old Glory juts
his lantern jaw toward the white-winged building where
    she hides terror
in tears, holding her braided, ribboned head as, between
    her ten-year-old
fingers, distorted clangor of malignant mob-voice
    penetrates with

curses and screams of coves and harpies, liquored-up
  looters, drink-mad,

blood-mouthed molls, ill-wind-shifted, now, toward
  Mary in the white-winged
Colored Orphan Asylum on Fifth Avenue, the ghost-
  building, inside tall
wealth, that I can reach in five minutes from this great,
  gray library,
close my book and walk out into the Fifth Avenue
  festival of limousines
and be inside of its smoldering, ectoplasmic doors with
  the orphan children,
who are always poorest, with Mary, who hides under
  her bed, her eyes

spraying terror, shutting her ears to the Fourth of July
  or, now,
a week later, to the flag-bearing giant leading a mob
  through the present
affluent Fifth Avenue shoppers to *BOOM BOOM KILL
  THE NIGGERS
NO DRAFT KILL*, outside the library window on Fifth
  Avenue, inside of,
behind, through, the tremendous modern traffic stalled
  at red, frustrated,
Manhattan-honking. *KILL!* Mary sees feet, fast feet.
  She doesn't

understand that the children are being herded out to
  safety, to
Blackwell's Island on the East River. Mary sees feet

scurry by her bed, sees a watery world, like one sub-
    merged, when she
looks out. Then, above her bed, something huge and
    malignant appears,
something too big. An evil thing! She will not come out
    from under, she will
not, as the white-winged building shakes like her body
    with battering

and the doors are pulled from their hinges. Mary tries
    to find her mother
inside of herself, and finds an entrance and a dark hall.
    She goes in,
finds herself upright, her legs steady under her. She
    pats the bodice
of her pink dress, straightens her pink ribbon—for she
    knows her mother
waits at the end of the dark hall—as the giant lifts her to
    the sky—
knows a door will open at the end of the dark hall—and
    dashes her ten-

year-old body down. Great doors open, her mother
    shimmers with beauty,
with long, strong, brown open arms. In fury at his loss,
    the giant howls
after the escaping orphans, and flames rise up around
    him as he moves,
touching, touching the pitiful beds of orphans, touching
    and torching,
his small mad head hissing, spitting curses upon
    Lincoln, the top-

hatted ape, and Greeley, and niggers, niggers, for his
   tongue would fork

with curses if it could, as the white-winged asylum
   crumbles
in flames inside of the facades of now with its *BEEP*
   BEEP of prosperity.
As if the great library walls had vanished, as if the
   market values of now,
with their multi-millions of construction, were trans-
   parent, there
stands the Colored Orphan Asylum, and there inside is
   Mary, hiding under
her bed. Mary and the flag-bearing giant. Mary and the
   mad mob. I lean

back in my library chair and push up my glasses. I am
   trying to see more
clearly. I think I don't understand any more than Mary
   did,
as the lion-braced library walls form around me again,
   shutting me off
from my shopping, struggling fellow Americans on
   Fifth Avenue, outside,
who cannot see the white-winged Colored Orphan
   Asylum as they pass it.
But I know that all hurts must be outlived as humanity
   presses forward.

OBITUARY
Edwin Marsh Schorb, Sr. (1893-1963)

> *Success is counted sweetest*
> *By those who ne'er succeed.*
> *—Emily Dickinson*

Without the mummeries of death, by fire,
but not by burning but by breath of smoke,
you died like some high god upon his pyre:
O quick, barbaric, merciful good luck!

I had so many fears for you, my father;
your ribald binges must have racked your body;
I feared some lingering illness, and I'd rather
have anything attacking one so bawdy

than an unthrilling, invalided life
spent somehow to its end in spite and temper;
though there was one thing sterner than its strife:
no death, no anything could make you whimper!

Your life was preparation for its pain:
you trained for ill and not for good, as Housman
advised his blear-eyed Shropshire lad to train
when, "moping melancholy mad," that yeoman

had rhymed the cow to death. A country boy
yourself, of Dutch and Anglo-Saxon stock,
New Jersey born and bred, hobbledehoy
and shining-faced, at fourteen, to New York

you went, in Nineteen-Hundred-Seven, to be
a runner on the New York Stock Exchange:
No more a rube!—No more a nonentity!—
but now (or then) a Wall Street runner, plung-

ing through the frantic, money-making crowds
America's romantic myth had brought
to conquer fortunes (time, events, becloud
so far-bygone an era, the magic sort

of moment that it was, the innocence
of fledgling fortune-hunters like yourself,
whose world of thought was Yankee common sense
and industry, who dreamed a sweet success

sometimes into existence in a trice:
opposing Mogul, Robber-baron, Tycoon,
all those first-comers who had set the price
of your success so high, O youngest son!)

Your struggle was a long one: studying
beside a late oil-lamp, O handsome youth
with raven hair!—your eyes only seeing
great dreams—reading of Rome, in law—in faith

that "Education makes the man;" with knowledge,
as Bacon'd put it, being power. Your roommate,
a brilliant graduate of Harvard College,
who one day would become a diplomat,

and later on Ambassador-at-large
in a long dead administration, instructed
you in "polish," as if you were his charge:
"Marry a rich woman," he told you once, "Ed.

That's my advice to you. I mean to do it
myself." Indeed, that's what he did. Not you,
though. Women meant too much. They knew you
   knew it,
too, handsome twenty-one, bonds salesman now,

and "Coming," as they called it then; they knew,
and loved you for it; helped you to establish
your reputation on The Street, and strew
themselves like flowers at your feet, flashing

their smiles like diamonds, their gems like teeth,
attracting and repelling, always rich
and husbanded by ghosts—a jewelled wreath
of Marley'd widows, beauties, and rich bitches,

young and old, fell about your frail young shoulders
—the day was almost won for Trumpery!
But meanwhile now the world was hurling boulders
of War, had been since Ferdinand, Humpty-Dumpty

of Peace, had fallen from the caving wall
at Sarajevo, four trenched and bloody years
before—time now for you to heed the call!
You went with other would-be "Officers

and Gentlemen" to be inducted, and
trained in the arts of martial leadership;
but suddenly, amazingly, they hand-
ed you your discharge.—We had won, had whipped

King Billy and the Ottoman Empire
(for better or for worse the deed was done!)

—and you, handsome young E.M. Schorb, Esq.,
were free to enter stormy Prohibition,

that time of Ought-not, But, and All-be-damned,
when "bathtub was synonymous with gin;"
an Eighty-nine-day-wonder, you had lammed
back into mufti—lost the veteran's pension

for my dear mother's Merry Widowhood;
but not your fault—a bureaucratic trick
that politicians played on Motherhood
is what we'll call it, for a sad laugh's sake.

Your first wife was a dopefiend. She's long dead.
The next an upright nurse—good family;
tubercular, although Bermuda bred;
and oh, British to the bone; unamatory,

or so you said, although you got a son
by her;—but not in Colorado, where
you went to help her lungs, and met someone
more amatory—Governor's daughter

she was: young, bright, and burning in her britches:
Black-Bottoming and Charlestoning and being
filled with a Flapper's ripe and bitching itches
—until you ran away from both of them.

By now you'd made the magic book—*WHO'S WHO*.
Success had come. You worked out of New York
and lived "Uptown"—and then the Market threw
its curve: Black Tuesday, Twenty-nine. What work

of evil genius had occurred? O fell
green hand of money! Lost hey-days! Your wife
was gone! Your son was gone, taken. What Hell
had happened and had happened here? What grief?

When, still young, you rode the Elevated,
the rumble of the wheels ground down your heart:
that iron-roar made you think quick death was fated,
thuswise against ambition raised your guard.

From then on you'd inveigh against that world
of Business, Finance, Property, Possessions
that you were trained in. Overboard you hurled
it, calling afterwards impedimenta

whatever slightest trinket stuck to you
as to summer-melting wax, which washed away
itself,—before the pierce-eyed public view!—
whatever'd stuck. The haberdashery

was all you kept: the custom-tailored suit;
silk tie; the Homburg hat; the shining shoes:
as you had worn them through the Prohibition Toot
you wore them through the sad Depression Days;

the Fylfot-War; the Eisenhower Fifties . . .
when I was there to know you, aging father:—
I, growing up by then, you in your sixties,
hair briny with the years, a heavy breather,

but still a regal, leucomelanous head—
bared now ("The man who never wears a hat"

was what they called you then—you were ahead
of time, before the style, an old pace-set-

ter—Kennedy would make bare heads official
—"My reason is to save my head of hair;
hats stop the circulation," you said; "this'll
become the style, when people learn.") Never

will I forget those idiosyncratic
quirks, those oddnesses, that set you apart
from ordinary beings so dramatic-
cally! I, walking by your side in Newark,—

where we then lived, deep in a basement flat,
where roaches climbed the walls like living paper,
and damp night brought the rustle of a rat,
—would glow to see the people look, O happier

than a rich son, to be the son of one
so striking and distinguished in appearance!
"That gent I seed you wid, are you his son?"—
yet of the poor we were among the poorest!

You'd married Mom in Nineteen-Thirty-Two,—
one year before Repeal, deep in Depression
days. Having met in a speakeasy, you
decided to continue partying—

and did throughout the years, by fits and starts!
Though making money was a difficulty
that interfered with freedom, your free hearts
went on their merry way, higgledy-piggledy,

from the Honeymoon Hotel, here in New York,
where you escaped the bill by wearing all
your wardrobe out the door, until the stork
dropped in your lap a wet, if "Wonderful!"

responsibility—which you were not
quite ready to live up to, though you tried—
"To be father, now! Why, I've forgot-
ten how to burp a child! I'm forty-five!"

Soon fifty-five! Now, door-to-door, you sold:
bandaids, thread, pots and pans, encyclopedias
(once more you carried Bacon's quote in bold
lettering on a business card, *KNOWLEDGE*

IS POWER!)—Oh, a library of books!
Ah, melancholy-morbid! How you read
"The Raven," with your Barrymorish looks
to help you dramatize as you recited!

And "To the Ladies!" How that angered Mom!
You made her Judy O'Grady, not the Lady,
while you remained the Colonel! Deaf and dumb
with anger, she would wait until payday

before she made things up. The years went by.
You went to work at managing hotels
for some cheap chain; then later you would try
your hand at selling real estate; but selling

was too rough now, Old Charmer, sixty-five!
And then you read De Quincey and De Ropp:

"Why, I have never even been alive!"
And that was how you found your way to dope!

To dope and death as well! For you left home,
went to a hobo rooming house downtown,
and, three weeks later—dead! O poor poor Mom!
"I loved him. Understood him? No." She frowned.

SIX DEAD IN BLAZE IN NEWARK, the paper said:
I read the headlines on the Hudson Tube
while on my way to Newark. Could you be dead?
Yes, I identified you at the Morgue!

Without the mummeries of death, by fire,
but not by burning but by breath of smoke,
you died like some high god upon his pyre:
O quick, barbaric, merciful good luck!

LETTERS HOME

(An R.A.F. Pilot, Bermudan, Age 21; 1943)

I am on standby at flights,
or flying from ten until ten.
That's from the A.M. to A.M.

I return in the morning and sleep
until tea-time, get up and have tea,
and then see a cinema show.

After the flicks I walk back,
go to mess, and to bed about ten.
So at long last I'm on operations.

I enclose the newspaper clipping
to show you my handiwork.
I got the two hits dead amidships.

God, I was thrilled! But don't think
that I gloat on the enemy dead—
just glad that I wasn't afraid.

The Maltese are marvelous people,
always so cheerful and smiling.
They really deserve the George Cross.

The hotel at which I am billeted
is situated on the sea front
at Sliema, so when I wake mornings

I can look out my window and see
the white Mediteranean waves
on water as blue as Bermuda's.

*Over sea, out of Tunis, past Sicily,
off Naples, their Wellington fell.
They took to their rubber dinghy*

*and had drifted for thirty-nine hours
when the Italians reported them down.
The Germans, at last, picked them up.*

(A Fellow Prisoner to the Pilot's Mother)

Madam, any attempt at escape
is infused with a great deal of danger,
the success of it usually being

more a matter of luck than design.
It so happened that I had myself
been preparing to make an attempt

when he came to me late on the eve
of his transfer by train from the camp.
I did not have the chance that he did,

so it seemed like the right thing to do
to surrender my maps and my compass
and whatever provisions I had.

His journey commenced in the morning.
When it showed itself likely to end
before darkness could cover his flight,

he decided to make his escape
in the full light of day, at first chance.
Now to jump from a train in the dark

is an orthodox mode of escape,
but to make such a break in broad day
involved so much greater a risk.

But your Jimmy accepted that risk.
As his train was held up in a station

he was able to knock out his guard

and to leap out and run down the platform.
But the guards in the other compartments
saw, and repeatedly fired.

(A British Nurse to the Pilot's Mother)

The cemetery is outside the town,
so was saved from the worst battle scars.
When I found it this morning, my dear,

your young Jimmy's sad grave was at peace
and had flowers, carnations and roses,
which were left there by persons unknown.

The Italians erected a stone
with his name and the date of his death
and the fact of his being a pilot,

but unfortunately this was toppled
by some bombs which had landed nearby.
Two young Tommies were visiting graves

and they helped me to prop the stone up,
and we took several photos beside it
which I'll forward as soon as developed.

Now the padre has promised to make
a large white wooden cross
and to put on it "Outerbridge, James,"

and the crest of the R.A.F.
and that he was born in Bermuda.
He isn't alone among strangers.

There are Yanks and Canadians, too.
It's a beautiful spot, with the sea,
like the sea of Bermuda, in sight.

(From His Last Letter)

. . . My Rhodes at Oxford is waiting,
so I study my Latin and Greek.
American sports are the thing,

and I play at softball every day
and am keeping quite physically fit.
You can learn almost anything here,

from chess to trombone playing,
and my program is so well arranged
that I haven't a moment to spare. . . .

But this last letter wasn't received
until more than a year after he
had been killed. It had obviously

travelled through many countries,
for it bore seven censorship stamps,
including the swastika.

SHARP

Poet of Parris Island

"Cock crows, wolf bays, caterwauls, eldritch sounds
  ringing out and echoing
    back from the escarpment, weird screams meant to
    terrify, crazily
announcing attack across fogbound spiderwebs of
  barbed-wired
    terrain. Then the poop of mortars, the red spit of
    burps,
a flare, shedding chartreuse in its lazy swaying gravity
  fall,
    beautiful tracers burning out in air, phosphorous
    grenades making

small midnight suns . . ."   Buck Sergeant Robert E. Lee
  Sharp of Macon read
    to his captive audience of Marine recruits his poems
    of Korean
conflict—recruits who had, night before, waded the
  blind-dark swamp of the
    Sea Island called Parris, shitbirds and turds up to
    their chins in
swamp gunk, whipped on and kicked by water mocca-
  sins, Mae-Wested
    in the dark by boa constrictors, or so they believed.
    All but Clover—

descendant of Sea Island plantation slaves, cursing the
  mouthfuls

of swampwash in gurgling Gullah, the islands' lingo
   —who knew the snakes
would be scared off by such commotion as this—two
  hundred-some farm
    boys and city slickers scared spineless in the snakes'
     swamp—knew
it was drowning to be feared, in the slippery dark, bur-
  dened with
    fifty-pound packs rifles helmets cartridgebelts can-
     teens bayonets and night-

blind eyes, under a starproof vegetable roof of shingling
  fronds and fans.
    Clover stretched his neck like a turtle above the din
     of clanks
splashes and shouts of terror. And always above any
  din Sharp's mellifluous
    Georgian, urging, commanding a motley crew of
     shitbirds and turds to become
Marines, who himself was Poster-Marine, whose men
  thought him perfect
    but for the fact that he was mad as the Hatter,
     perfect, but for

his constant, barely submerged violence, which was the
  song behind his words
    now, as he read with great beauty, vivid clarity, his
     martial
poems of nightmare mayhem on Bunker Hill and
  Snipers Ridge, where
    he won a chestful of medals, a seemingly mad hero
     Marine poet

drill instructor, angrier than God. At what? War, the
    poems told, at war,
        at human nature, at himself, filled with his own
        violence; at us, too,

but to save us, always to make us triumph over what he
    had endured, cried:
        "Coming! Outposts in! The sand-bagged weight of
        the bunker collapsed
under artillery—a full barrage—pf-f-f-f-f BOOM—and
    the Reds slid
        in on us. Got one under my arm and slit his throat.
        Now tell me about
Mao, I said; *I'll tell you about freedom, you two-*
    mouthed bastard!" Sharp scanned
        us, in our skivvies on the squadbay floor, across the
        little table he

brought to his recitals. "Unnerstay-end," he growled,
    "Mr. Kennan in
        Washington has devised for America a policy of
        containment. The Reds
cain't continue to eat if they don't swallow up other
    countries. They don't
        create wealth, they re-dis-tri-bute it. Get me? They
        are an empire.
Unnerstay-end what that is? They gotta eat up their
    neighbors
        or else they collapse. Unnerstay-end? Do you
        dumb shitbirds

unnerstay-end what it's all about, what Bunker Hill was
    about—either

one?   About FREEDOM, you dumb turds,
    FREEDOM! You eat enough 'gator-
doo, you'al'll learn. One o' them Reds shoots your
    balls off—Non
    emasculatatum est—"   Off in another reality field,
    Sharp whispers, "My
best buddy, from Valdosta . . ."   Back. "You gonna
    priss like girls when you march.
    We gonna win the base ensign. I don't care a fid-
    dler's bitch if the

red flag goes up at a hunnerd-ten degrees. You gonna
    priss like girls.
    You gonna look PRETTY. Get me?   And you know
    what you gonna be?
Do you?   You gonna be God bless America Uncle
    Sam's most perfect killers.
    Now what you gonna be?"   *SIR, killers, SIR!* "Makes
    my heart sing.
And if the army and the navy ever get to heaven's scene
    . . . What, dammit?"
    They will find the streets are guarded by United
    States Marines, SIR!

PART FIVE

MOONTIME

The Greeks measured Earth by its shadow on the moon. Thoreau said, Time is a stream I go fishing in. Ford said, History is the bunk. Sumerian writing, done on clay tablets, shows about 2000 pictographic signs. The moon is a bad woman because she is very romantic. We all know the trouble romance can get you in. I am romantic tonight, amorous with the moon. O how many leaves lay scattered? I guess thousands, and I have a study that agrees with me. When you pay for a study, you get what you want. Therefore, all studies are romantic and have a dark side like the moon. Theodora, the Byzantine empress, died in 548, one of a kind. Her death was a big relief to some of her subjects. Five years later disastrous earthquakes shook the entire world. The house I live in was built much later. I leave the actual count to you. The first water-driven mechanical clock was constructed in Peking in 1090, the wrist watch around the turn of the Twentieth century. I've got a digital that I can read in the dark. I can also read the chained and sailing moon from here. Its glyphs of pox say the odds are against us.

THE IDEOLOGUES:
OR, THE TWENTIETH CENTURY REVISITED

> *Embrace the butcher, but*
> *change the world . . .*
> —Bertolt Brecht: The Measures Taken

Brecht

Pound

Brecht

What to say of them?

Why to say it?
Because they have given and taken importantly.
Because they have helped humankind and hurt it.

The two of you.

At what point does it become apparent,
even to genius,
that means must be golden,
that means are the only end?

Bert,
Ezra,
think of Confucius
whom you both so admired.

When you embrace the butcher

you embrace dead meat,
Brecht,

Pound.

Brecht,
never when mad murderous Uncle Joe
purged did you utter revulsion.
You knew your Hobbes, knew human nature.
You'd met the Kremlin himself.
You knew it was power not people he loved.
And later
after the rising of the 17th June
53 when the workers were shot in the Stalinallee
and the Soviet tanks rumbled again in Berlin
and you submitted,
submitting your letter supporting Ulbricht
and the censors erased every word you had written
but your statement of Socialist Party attachment
and you guiltily dreamed of fingers of workers
pointing you out,
did you wistfully wish that the State
would wither away?
And Pound,
not till Benito swung by his jackbooted
hobnailed heels
did you quit.
Not till they stopped you.

The measures taken embraced the butcher,
Brecht,
Pound,

odd duo,
Spartans,
seeking the hideous Platonic perfection,
the Toolmaker's State,
to make a machine of the human condition,
an ideology of deus ex machina.

Here are your jacks-in-the-box of Pandora:
sad angry young Schicklgruber,
failure of failures,
architect of frustration,
Der Führer, king of kitch,
more of a murderous joke
than Chaplin could make him,
Capo di Capi
of Benito, himself no bundle of joy;
and Joe Dzugashvili,
Stalin,
self-styled "Man of Steel."
Mere murderers, the three of them.

Brecht,
didn't you notice the comic-book element?
Pound,
what of the jackboots,
the leather?
Didn't you heed the automaton goosestep?
Poets,
didn't you listen to the demagogic language?
But the ends justify
what,
dynamic duo?

The death of millions?
Hitler, hater of Jews,
Stalin, murderer of Mandelstam
for a printed reproof,
Benito, jackbooted journalist,
the three of them: murderers.

Where is the golden omelet they made?
The living became the dead,
the left wing and the right
wing are the feathery dead
and the fool's-golden bird in ashes.
To rise again?
Always,
always,
sadly, a phoenix of filth.
Whom, what, to blame?

Not the disorder of slow trains,
not the criminal economics of Versailles,
nor alas in the name of God or goodness the Jews,
but ourselves,
our soulless, soul-seeking selves,
ourselves,
the paranoids,
the schizoids,
for hearing voices,
voices of comic-book heroes,
men-of-steel,
ourselves who sanction action,
sociopathic action,
hurrying history,

hurrying heaven-on-Earth,
the on-time trains,
the golden wheat of the Five-Year Plan,
that millennium of earthly dominion,
the Thousand-Year Reich,
so we can get on with it
and in on it,
before Time takes us to our soul's Nowhere,
disapproving love,
patience with human error,
failure, weakness,
tender Bert,
generous Ez.

For a theater, Bert!
For a microphone, Ez!
For a theater,
with your Austrian passport
and your West German publisher!
for a microphone,
with your half-baked hatred of Jews
and your crazy Social Credit!

Were you naive?
Were you mad?

For a theater!
And a mike!
For a playhouse
and a megaphone!
For an audience
and a pulled-up vanity,

Bert,
Ez,
you tender and generous poetic hopes
and tyrannical human disappointments!
When poets don't know any better
what is their use on this planet?

Plato would NOT
have banned you from his perfect State,
Brecht,
Pound,
and that's your disgrace,
you lessons to be learned,
you slaves to your own slaver,
you paladins of palaver!

Where is the end of murder?

Oh for the gay days of the Hitler-Stalin Pact!

For a playhouse
and a megaphone!
For a dollhouse
and a rolled-up newspaper!
Hurry history!
Hurry the Communist heaven,
the heaven-on-earth with the workers underfoot!
Hurry the Fascist heaven!
Hurry the race white as worms!
Hurry the Platonic,
the Ideal,
the Perfect,

the Procrustean,
hurry,
hurry,
hurry,
come and get it!

CODA: THE DIAMOND MERCHANT

A diamond is forever.
—B. J. Kidd

The buoys of memory have faint bells, noticed in the
    night.
I have left these chiming seamarks for the time of my
    return.
They ring out there, but faintly, so faintly I can hardly
    hear.
I think they want me to remember the severances of the
    soul,
if soul is more than mere electric tissue. If Death is
    king
and I do not reclaim what I have jettisoned, it goes to
    him.
I do not want the king to have my life. Therefore, each
    night at sea,
I must set out to find the ringing buoys and haul aboard
the lagan realities, for now my aging body, my
    emotional mal de mer,
lend renewed reality to the cold, damp camps. One
    numbered friend

should wear a wedding ring, another was engaged, and
   yet a third,
below and silent, had eyes like Tavernier blue diamonds set
   in Fabergé
eggshell by the master. I cannot put a name to the
   smiling face I see,
but she existed, who is now the faint dream of a
   denouement.

     Shalom alekhem   *Shalom alekhem*

So now I sail all night to find them and their symbols, to
connect with them whatever seems appropriate, their
   rings,
their eyes, their ways: but not alone to find the persons
but to find the meanings of the persons to myself, the
   electric
mind, before the king should claim them from my life.

THE JOURNEY

a symphonic poem

Lucid Dreams

I.

The Association for the Study of Lucid Dreams
summoned me to the Hotel Paradiso
to participate in a study in which I was to sleep
and be awakened while I was dreaming
and was to maintain my dream
and then to convert it
into whatever dream I wished it to become.

Lucid dreams are more vivid than common dreams.
Inscape is energized, so that the world of the dream
is like that of Hopkins or Van Gogh,
pulsating, dynamic, vital.
Such imagery is said to be
the manifestation of cosmic holograms,
and if I can convert them,
I can convert my life, like a wizard,
turn it into what I want it to be,
or wished it were or had become,
bring time back
with what and whom I loved, set a new
course for myself, and embark.

II.

I saw white gulls arise, upon arrival,
from the emerald maze in the huge garden
surrounding the Hotel Paradiso. White gulls.
Don't they always arrive with a ship,
following for her flotsam and jetsam?
And that night I dreamed I saw an instant,
which was a dewdrop in my dream,
yes, a dewdrop and a stellar instant,
like that of the wild gulls, pulling
the air with their wide wings,
an image, a vision of heavenly flight—
an ascent, a transcendence—
a nano-second and a shimmering drop,
or, shifting, a shimmering shield,
hovering in space, and what looked like
a moonbeam crossed the dark,
the silver dark of a swirling dust mote,
a hazed, illumined, impossible dark,
fingered, like a laser, touched the instant,
the drop, the Lilliputian planet,
with the most tender touch imaginable,
angling this way and that, so that
with each angle an entire eternal history was
displayed,
            with all of the mass and multiplicity of life.

It seemed in my dream that there was no death,
but a cottage-coziness everywhere, and of us
and of the mountains and the waters, seemed

that all these are projections of personality,
(what I see I see because I am I)
spiritual manifestations, tilts at the dewdrop,
incarnations and aspects of the All-in-all,
the anomalon itself, yes, and even that sheen,
that spark, on the oriflamme of time; seemed
that we are the one hologram of life,
and that the family portrait
is the portrait of all who ever lived,
with mountains and waters and creatures
wild and domesticated; seemed that
the holographic plate is angled
for this simulacrum, this three-dimensional portrait
of a universe-apparent, which portrait
is not a memento mori but a glory
in a turning in time, a journey around a star.

My dream suggested that behind my waking back
a deeper reality existed;
not the reality I saw before me,
amazing pattern that it is,
a life-long complicated quilt,
tangible, deep in its seams,
full in its bosomy pads; but another,
finer, more heavenly, fabric, a cloth-of-gold,
glorious, gorgeous, radiant beyond imagination
with a light unknown here, waves
in an intensity beyond experience,
yet that do no damage to the eye,
light that seems to love the eye—
and that is the Word, I thought,
with new insight: Love—which is

expressed in its star-stuff, its human
potential, but never for good and all,
for there is more, we feel certain, we who
are the stars singing, the vibratory expression
of matter, tuning fork to tuning fork,
the template of interference-patterns making
concentric intersecting rings until
with perfect pitch achieved
the magical-appearing universe
leaps into view—until the great music
is made tangible and a table and chairs
and a world and a universe, full of stars
to look at, from a cottage
in an enchanted wood,
where I sit, appear.

When, like a man with warlock vision,
I watch the wilted wonders of my past
parade in phalanx, I dream
that I can change my present state
by intervening there,
where those wonders are and now parade,
multiplicities of self, time-separated,
rude and naked strutting fools,
but now, with a maturing vision,
refreshed with vivid hope,
their formation ordered,
their banners held high,
becoming what they might have been,
myself in time where time must be to make a memory,
and invested with new direction,
can have them at command fall out

or turn about or right or left,
know they are free in paradox,
not locked forever there, in constant error—
yet go on, the same, as if my will
required my life—perhaps
some missing faith, perhaps some expiation.
Again perhaps the wonders are mirage
and I was born this very instant,
tilted to a history and told a fate.

These reality fields are open for inspection,
like model homes, and, in an augenblick,
we are visiting an infinity of them.
They are where you are,
you need not go to see them:
no agent is necessary. Intersecting
concentric rings are vibrating
everything into view. The reality fields
present glories and horrors to behold:
they are moral reflections, purifying
the spirit, cleansing the dewdrop,
keeping it clear and clean, all
that I love borne with me
through time and back out of it,
the lovelight never out, always tilting,
becoming a new vision!

III.

But a Bodhisattva,
or even a Beverly Hills guru,

might say, might well say, did say:
"Dead flesh is mad with flies.
The world is mad with lies!"

When you are about three feet tall,
the gray streets of Philadelphia
in winter are very long and tiring
and slowly climb uphill toward a dark sky.
His mother pulled him along.
Where were they going?
Their arms were empty.
Not shopping?
Was there no money?
Why were they walking, walking so far?
He was beginning to get very cold.
Then, on the deserted street,
a stranger appeared before them.
His mother knew the man,
yes, and they laughed together, startling laughter,
too high above him for him to have any idea
what was funny, but something obviously was,
for their laughter tinkled down upon him
like sprightly snowflakes, like tinsel and sequins,
a glittery sprinkling of fairy dust.
He tried to get under it, between them, where it fell.
His mother pulled him back and away,
toward her own back.
Then the man seized his mother
in his arms and dipped her back
toward where he waited,
and kissed her hard and long.
It was wrong, wasn't it?

Because this man was not his father.
His father was up ahead somewhere,
somewhere at the end of the long gray avenue,
somewhere up several flights of stairs,
in a small flat that looked down on the avenue,
drinking. It was wrong, wasn't it? Because
his mother did not struggle to be free.
Instead, she simply held him behind her,
away from them. He thought he might cry.
The man seemed to lift his mother
off the pavement
and to place her back on it,
her high heels firm.
She pulled him from behind her
and around to her side,
her other hand held out to the man
as he stepped back, back,
and turned and went a little way,
and stopped, and turned again,
and waved, and blew her a kiss,
and turned once again,
and went on down the long slowly sinking avenue.
Who was that? he wanted to know.
His mother pulled him forward up the hill.
"Who was that man?" he asked.
His mother climbed on,
pulling him along with one hand
and wiping tears from her eyes with the other.
"Mommy, who was that man?"
His mother ignored him until he shouted his question at
    her.
The question and its answer had become imperative,

like the bearing down of traffic at the intersection.
Finally his mother said, "What man?"
He looked back and saw the receding figure
of the man who had kissed his mother,
no more than a dot now, a dot in time.
He tugged his mother half around and pointed—
"That man," he said.
"I don't see any man," his mother said.
"I haven't seen anyone since we began our walk,
and neither have you."
He looked back again, desperately,
but the man was gone, only eternity,
only infinity remained to see. "You see,"
said his mother, "there is no one
on the street but us."
She was lying, wasn't she,
or could he not believe
the evidence of his own eyes?
From then on he struggled
to keep his hand free of hers.

Memory, or lucid dream?
This hologram-like universe
seems solid, appears to have parts, can be
taken apart—(I, too, am like a child and
love a stack of gears)—so we take it apart,
emotionally, mechanically, mathematically,
take it apart as children will a watch,
begin to conceive of it as a watch, as Voltaire
did (and generously gave it a Watchmaker),
and become convinced that it is a kind of watch.
We lift out structures, sequences, relationships,

and rearrange them, and they become to us
what we have come to believe they are—
ballbearings unto infinity.

Answers generate questions in the mechanical sphere:
the universe expands, more complicates itself.
We are made to ask and so increase
dimension, to multiply dimensions, to make the
picture greater, more inclusive of the non-existent,
to take back the ghosts and reinvest them,
to live again in the mirage, to beat the golden soul
so fine it floats and flutters like a translucent gauze.
The impulsion to think is part of the expansion itself,
and we must think like messenger-angels,
in a completeness of service, or we confuse ourselves
and take the wrong turn, and miss the point—
shall we say the dewdrop—at which
courage and intelligence and praise
meet, and await us.

The Poet

I.

Poetry possesses the virtue of being a record,
and you can date a poem, if you wish,
thus giving it the merit of a worldly fact
contained in a system of time, which, admittedly,
is a system which is perhaps pseudo-fact itself,
or will become so as matter completes its withdrawal
upon itself to revisit its origins in a hole in space;

and yet, until then, something like a fact,
a fact in the sense that Sherlock Holmes is almost real
and lives at 221-B Baker Street in a fictional series
in a real world that may exist only in a dream
that is being dreamed elsewhere, perhaps by God,
perhaps by the clever Its of Else in Otherwhere;
and so poetry becomes an actual little stab
and, poets hope, rip in the black sheet
that covers the deserted, haunted mansion.
> *In many moods,*
> *the poet broods,*
> *on dice and swans*
> *or old bygones,*

the hurts of a lifetime piling at the poet's knees,
the joys stacking under the poet's chin,
and should the poet be deceived, what of it?
The created icons of the poet's labor remain, untrue
perhaps to truth but true enough to themselves,
like Doctor Watson waiting for Holmes at 221-B Baker
   Street,
the poems piling like paintings or statuary, marking
the poet's being there, the idiosyncratic spelling the
   poet's own,
the music the sweet strain of the poet's soul
asking the rhetorical questions of the poet's life,
the unanswerables called eternal questions, the poet
insisting upon the attempt, one more human attempt,
which the poet was made for, wondering about
> *new turns of fate*
> *in love and hate,*
> *or what wild words*
> *are sung by birds.*

My little rubber doll Mickey melted in the hot trunk the summer
I was five, and I lost my only friend, his brown rubber hair a smear.
  I was very lonely without Mickey so I got a cat named Winkey but
  I didn't know how to spell that so I renamed her Scuttlebutt,
which I could spell believe it or not because of a character
in a cartoon in the Sunday funny pages somewhere but I don't know
where we were living then—we were usually on the go.
  I think my father was running from the law or from his first wife
  or both—he drank a lot, maybe he was just running from his life
—anyway I recall going up and down in the world and to and fro.
Being an only child and being poor with parents who are drunk a lot
of the time is a good way to develop one's ability to plot,
  so I began to draw and write a comic strip called Kid Danger,
  about a motorcycle cowboy who was always out to lasso a gangster
and who had a magical friend who I believed was a Hottentot,
because I had read something about them in the *Wonder*

Book of Knowledge
(which itself stood me in good stead later when I went
   to college)—
      and he wore the clothing of the black man in the
         book and a turban
      and had more dignity than the other seven or even
         the U'do Urban
and before he had joined Kid Danger he had been king
   of his village.
The plot thickened because the gangster became
   president of the US
of A, and Kid Danger and his Hottentot friend, whom
   he called Uziss,
      had to cope with the defending combined forces of
         the United States,
      and in one episode they were forced to storm the
         White House gates,
and I couldn't get the story straightened out and
   dropped the whole mess.
Anyway I was nearly ten by this time and I had to go
   out and work,
and my imagination began to fade away on the streets of
   Newark
      and pretty soon I forgot about Mickey and Winkey
         and Kid Danger
      and his friend Uziss the Hottentot and what should
         become of the gangster
and after many adventures pleasant and unpleasant I
   moved to New York.
But last night I dreamed of them all again, first one,
   then the other,
and sadness overwhelmed me when I thought of my

melted Mickey who was like a brother
   and my cat Winkey or Scuttlebutt and Uziss the
   Hottentot and Kid Danger
   and how I could never show them how finally to
   catch that gangster,
and I sat on linoleum roses again and cried, seeing my
   poor father and mother.

II.

In trying to discover the source of pain,
the poet, strange researcher into reality,
dipso-dreamer, lover of passion fruit,
unhappy hedonist of heterodoxy,
explores the familiar territory of the heart—
nothing but red caves and periodic floods.
He then travels up his plaque-clogged carotid
to the brain and comes upon a land of gray clouds
capped by a bone-pale dome. Under those
electrically-charged gray clouds, he listens
as the dome reverberates with the tom-tom beat of
"Worship me," and "Worship me."
I think I am getting close to the source of pain,
he tells himself. But it is only a false start,
a Lake Tanganyika. This cannot be the source
of the Nile of Pain. Here he is attacked by Synapses,
who pitch fiery assagais upon him without regard
for his gifts; he surrenders and they make him their
   slave.
What to do? He must escape if he is ever to find
the source of pain—which is now active in his heart.

He gives the gift of full worship to the King of the
     Synapses,
who drinks blood and eats oxygen, and,
for the gift of his blood, his oxygen, is set free
to go on looking for the source of pain.
He travels over rough, cortical country,
dead cells adrift in offshoot rivers and rivulets
of his previous life's best cognac, until, at last,
he comes to what appears to be a veritable
Victoria of a lake, an inland sea, too large to measure
with his meager instruments of sound and sense.
It is paradisiacal, even Heavenly,
for brightness shows down now
from the dome of Sunday. This is indeed
the source of Pain, for it is the citadel of sad desire;
and it is then and there that he makes
his most astounding discovery: to wit,
that in leaving this place, pain begins to flow
and flows on until it reaches the fell Falls of Destiny,
and, undeterred, goes over the falls in a barrel,
the inside of which is stained and caked
with the lees of the grapes of wrath.
He awakens on a Bowery-of-the-mind,
in a lake of golden pee, none-the-worse,
nor better, for his adventure,
but his mouth dry as a marrowless bone.

This makeshift shadowy world is metaphor,
        which is our chariot of choice,
     our light-inducting dark-proof vehicle
ready to ride the road and river of space and time,

to deliver us from evil,
which is all that isn't in the vision
of the cloud-bodied hungry soul
when it goes through the gate to the mystery
of unanswering love,
and we see from there how all things flow
outward toward wisdom
and back upon themselves toward joy
and that love is always answering,
is the cloud formed into self,
which is others and all, at once.

The Shade

I.

I would rejoin myself, deserted long ago,
that wandering shade somewhere in its separate time.
They say that the spirit hovers above the body while we
    sleep
and if we awaken suddenly we are dazed until it returns.
I would rejoin my earliest remembrance and start anew.
Travelling warily all roads,
I would be a dangerous companion for the unwary,
a disturbance in the calm weather of thought.
But that shade, transparent as an angel fish,
luminous at night as the moon on a mote of dust,
O, the lost bodiless distant song of that shade!
What wilderness of calm does it wander
bravely seeking the way home to chaos?

II.

There was a time when no season prevailed,
when whatever season it presumed itself to be
held no distinction: day and night fell too
into the inconsequential: all units failed,
for they failed in the beholder, the keeper of time:
and all distinctions faded, for the beholder
could not distinguish one thing from another.
The curious will ask how this occurred.
This much we know: that there was love
gone wrong, and there was death, death
of one most beloved—all share the news—
and there was inability produced, nurtured,
by the particular way of the life itself:
but even before these triggers, fast and slow,
were pulled, the life had been filled with walls
within which lurked the known fear
and beyond which lurked the unknown fear.
And the child's head had been early cloaked
in a liripipe, shut about the eyes
as dark as blindness: and the mind,
in its strange bonehouse, dwelt,
trying to see into and through the dark.
That is the state in which we feel little,
avoid sensations of pain or joy
through the medium of an inner mechanism
not fully understood. In this state
we seem to be neither living nor dead,
but existing without sensation,
seemingly dead, while still experiencing

some state of being approximating to life,
like the dream-state of the butterfly soul
that we experience in sleep, or, say,
the vague state of life of the slug or worm,
and we are sometimes found to be
existing in this manner as the result
of our inability to cope with the life
we have been living. It is as if
the transmigratory process had been
frustrated, leaving the victim in limbo,
neither able to progress nor to regress
to a previous state, like death but not death,
like life but not life as the living know it,
merely a camelopard likeness of it,
cataleptic, painless and joyless. Patience
is called for in such cases. Kindness helps
to undo harm, but the victim
will awaken only when ready.

III.

The dying Greek Egyptologist,
my fellow guest and subject of study,
spoke in his hypnotized sleep.
The group, bat-eared, heard
his inner voice, a *cri de coeur*,
from the garden with its green
labyrinth, like a sea-wind.
We were there to understand.
We were there to change our fate.

Where did the parting begin?
Why did the soul of the boy go away?
How has the man made his father and mother?
Why is his flesh like androgynous clothing?
What is the meaning of being oneself?

The dying Greek says that he cannot tell
the horn from the ivory, the true from the false.
"The world is mad with lies.
I do not think that I shall die."
Nonetheless, an inner voice said,
and I think all of us heard that haunting voice—

I embarked from the black lava beaches of Thira
for deadly sun-jewelled Egypt.

The sirens of the dust,
did they sing me a new song,
did they pied-pipe my heart away?

Yes, Egypt is the only place to die.
There they know how to treat a soul.
There, when you go down,
you go down to go on,
if in another way.

Ask the dunes in the Valley of Death.

Speak to the Sphinx.

Ask at Alexandria.

The Greek has a terminal virus of some kind,
a growing vegetation of the brain.
A virus has more organized life than a star,
though a star has an order of appearance,
star in the sky and star on stage.
We have a famous film star with us—
è bell' attrice—addicted, suicidal.
Parmenides mentored Zeno to believe
in the unchanging universe
behind the changing one.
In Rome, the film star could only find
a scrolling phantom life, too unsubstantial
for her solid flesh. She sought *la dolce vita*
in drugs and now, three times removed
from her dream of life, she tries again
in the labyrinth of the Minotaur, unaware
that she is filming Beauty and the Beast.
But I am speaking of organic life,
though a star on the stage
or a movie star has organic life,
more, in fact, than the Greek's virus.
But humans are gaudy coelenterates:
my liver heaves, my bowels twist,
squirm with excitement
and lead their own lives inside me.
I need a new part. It flowers, pulsates.
It is not my friend, it is itself.
But perhaps we can get along, after a time.
At first, other parts reject it,
but eventually they are tamed.
You are all working for me, I cry.
We are our own liver, kidney, heart.

I am not your heart.
You have no heart.
Your better half told you that.
You have no other half.
It is all a golden fiction, inspired by sex.
Your sex organs aren't even your own—
they do as they please.
As the real estate agent told the homeowner
who questioned him about an easement,
you don't own property, you control it.
You don't own yourself, and you barely,
for social reasons, control yourself.
One anti-social day, a day my tenure
and my poems almost couldn't save me,
one mad and drunken day, I stripped
and ran around the campus flagpole,
a proud if pallid paladin. Wirra!

Life is the opposite of what is burning out there
in space, that celestial snow, those flickering fireflies,
which, close up, are all titanic violence.
Life is soft and squirms when you caress it,
and it could rule the night of the stars, if given time.
But I think of Earth as a great piñata, stuffed with death.
Traditionally, at the end of a fiesta,
you take a whack at a piñata and it breaks,
spilling its contents. If you did that with Earth,
the countless dead would be released
and scattered into space,
and, though the geologists
and the astrophysicists
would disagree with me,

I say that what would be left
would be a tenth the size of the present globe,
a wrinkled, raisin-like, bag that no longer had an orbit
or an axis on which to fall toward the sun
or to do its wobbly spin, not the shiny dewdrop that it is.
The dead from Earth's beginnings to the present,
or what was left of them,
would float off and become pinwheels,
shaped and braced by dark matter,
much as the stars, the galaxies, are floating off,
away from each other, red-shifted,
and growing lonelier and lonelier.
Stand in the midst of life
and look at them go, to bones, to smoke, to ashes;
then rejoin the matter of the universe yourself;
the universe that, if it were capable of hope,
could only hope to live.

IV.

I heard the calls again, through the long night,
material manifestations of the ghostly immaterial.
Or, if you are not of a fanciful turn of mind,
if you prefer the psychological explanation
for every sort of phenomenon,
it must have been the wind I heard,
and the hotel settling
(an ancient building creaks),
the water pipes gurgling,
the radiators knocking, the cats
in the garden, skulking,
and transformed these in my mind

into the calls I thought I heard
that sounded to me like the crying out
of the earth's multitudinous dead.
And what I felt they told me
of my life's unmeaning,
my time's misuse,
my soul's fear,
out of the vastness,
the great underdarkness,
caused me to writhe in my wet white sheets
and sweat, glistening, like a great, limbed worm.
I awakened, startled, and, finally, I slept again,
a victim of circadian rhythm,
and dreamed of the drab furnished rooms of my infancy,
the dismal corners occasionally shot with sunlight,
the fascinating dust swirls that were my first view of the
    universe.
O make me at last an Immortal born for this life,
so hard when the wind like a horse that has eaten of
    loco weed
kicks in the shining green meadow of death that is the
    bright day
beyond which the galaxies turn in dark matter like great
    carousels
with mad imagery rising and falling along their white
    ways,
all celestial combustion and anger as if there were truth
    in the gods
and I had come from their birth to mine that happened
    in heat
in the bowels of the ship of the universe powered by
    diamonds,

dead glitters of light burnt in the cones of the sky. O
  Heraclitean Fire,
forgive one who has not known the one pinch of peace
held in the index and thumb of the chef who concocted
  this terrible stew,
brew that biology seeks in its crystals that fall like the
  fall of each phylum
down the great day of time, no matter all time be an
  infinite cloud,
O Fire have mercy and snuff out the wick of your run-
  ning black wax
and spare me the waste of beginnings, evolutions, and
  ends.

STOP, stop, poor soul, for the fire at the center of self is
  the fire at all distances,
emanation and flow like the oceans of life serve
  likewise the Heraclitean Fire
though the walking world is of mercury sulphur and
  salt, sex sun and sand,
yet the fire heats the shards till they melt, reshaping
  them in their clay and
thereby a new entity is formed bearing the heart's
  evergreen name of Hope.

The Labyrinth

I.

Déjà vu is the constant companion of every twice-
  thinking poet.

One minute I was sitting on a dull linoleum rose,
watching the swirling dust motes with my toys,
and the next they were utterly lost to me,
travelling down the street in a brown paper bag
in a grinding garbage truck.
My musical sweet-potato was crushed and wheezing
in my mouth, and tears were spraying silver on gold
in the windowlight for my melted Mickey doll,
my only friend.
                              Yes, I am there—here—there!
But now I sit in a porcelain tub that smells of chlorine
    and soap,
pouring from a fifth, hearing the Fifth—
da-da-da-dum— da-da-da-dum—
frowning, frowning, for the bird's song,
or Death knocking—in a tiled room full of steam,
with no childhood left, an old man with a gray beard
and no toys but a cheap, green cigar.

When first I arrived at the Hotel Paradiso
and was elevated many levels and taken back down
and led through long halls of many mysterious doors
to the suite of the Association, I felt oppressed,
and the notion of an open labyrinth came to me,
I was so desirous of freedom, of escape,
and found myself wandering through such a labyrinth,
or maze changeable as a tour puzzle, in the garden,
one made of many walls of either hard matter,
compressed particles to stop the Minotaur,
or something else and softer, miraculously
drawn into the continuum, perhaps hedgerows,
greens of light and dark hues in hearted leaves

and dimensionalized by back-shadows
of sunstruck and ever-variable mauve.
Beneath my feet were gravity's flagstones,
embedded in endless grains of sand,
and above my head mindless undisciplined
cloud formations backed by a dream of blue.

The open labyrinth my mind had conjured
was not a place to get completely lost in,
nor in which a quarantine prevailed.
There others step out of nowhere, or seem to,
because the labyrinth has spaces for crossing
from one side of its elusive walls to the other,
with many signs pointing the way out. And yet
we remain lost, we remain lost even as we are given
exact directions. Why? Why is this the case?
Because we do not want to leave the open labyrinth,
even though we are becoming famished
for what is outside it, which well might be
a void. Politely, we listen to directions
we are given, then go another way,
hoping that wherever we go will lead us
deeper than ever into the heart of the maze.
And even so, we advise others on how to escape.
And our advice is exact, for we know how to escape.
We know that we need do nothing at all but wait,
with an immense show of patience, here or there,
this side or that.
                        But truly we have no desire to leave,
for all our hopes and fears are here where we wander,
aimlessly, aimlessly but full of purpose.

II.

I read somewhere about a wizard with computers,
a man who's made a myriad millions in the field,
who lives out in an island's perfect solitude
in order best to think about life's origins,
who seriously thinks our universe is bits
and bytes, a program made some cosmic Otherwhere.
   We make computer games ourselves and love to play
      them,
why then might we not be a game for something else,
a smarter It, why might it not be true that we,
the world, the universe, are toys played in an Else,
a game called Life, or its equivalent in Else,
played by the happy children of the clever Its?
   Truly the Demon of Intelligence must thrive
among the happy Its of Else in Otherwhere,
but one must notice all the cruelty of the game
and think that those in Else have not evolved as yet
to that high point that even we, their bits and bytes,
their pawns, aspire to daily in our average lives.
   I must look up that article about the wizard
and find his name and write to him and ask him how
he thinks the whole thing works, and if the software
      used
is durable enough to keep us going on until
our progress takes us well beyond the happy Its
of Else in Otherwhere, who play such cruel games.

III.

For breakfast at the Hotel Paradiso
a wrinkled yellow passion fruit is served.
Judging from the taste of it, there's paradise inside,
and juice of it must be the rivers, lakes, and seas
of such a place that could produce a native
whose perfume turns the head of each new traveler
   there
and makes of him a siren's hind, a slave
of persons of the place, one who is so compelled,
entrapped, that that awed visitor would never leave,
would think it madness to travel after smelling
compelling sweetness on a vivid gust;
judging from the taste of it,
paradise could be described as what we all
most dream of goodness wished for in that safest place
the heart can find, where, unafraid of anything,
we ask for what we truly want—
that which we dare not hint before—
and then are more than satisfied,
and soonest, and most easily.
O judging from the taste of such sweet fruit,
there truly is a paradise and all we wish is deep inside
   it—
the life, the love, the death.

It is this heavenly tale,
that the child in one could wish for,
that keeps me awake tonight,
on the eve of my departure,
fearing death and wishing for grace,
not knowing what either is,

or even if either is,
though the unbreathing stillness of bodies
has me fairly convinced of the former,
and of the latter I have seen so little
as to doubt what I have seen as aberrant,
some twist in the air and light that,
so full of desire for the magic of exemption,
I have deluded myself, half knowing I lied,
half believing my own white lie.

But by now I've come to believe
that the only grace
is the goodness of the rational mind,
and the only evil
the old instinctive animal brain,
the knob of the cerebellum,
seeking its own satisfactions
of food and sex and selfhood,
the ultimate isolate one,
that yet does not understand
that we are together
in this flowing, amazing hologram,
with or without a creator
that may or may not care;
that, come to consciousness,
we have every right to judge
the nature of existence, for,
however arrived at, our brains
are analytic, not made to hunker down
in obeisance to riddling gods,
nor to any phantom
                    that hides in a cloud of unknowing.

For we have one another and
have courage and the hope of courage and
the practice of courage, to help us,
and, when the wind is calm,
and the waters lean down for the moon,
we have lonely senses to share
till at last our time has run out.

Now, as I think in the night,
somewhat afraid of the day
that will see me another day older
and that much closer to death,
I mark the speed of time
that has seen me, a moment ago,
a child walking home from school,
or a man going off to harm's way,
or this or that or the other,
and think of these things that we have,
of others and courage and love,
and I think that I'll sleep and awaken
less anxious than I was considering
a heavenly tale,
                    for in the realest reality,
the closest thing to the truth,
there is finally a peace of mind
that is a grace in a sweet surrender.
It is the heavenly tale
that the child in one should wish for.
It will allow me to sleep
on the eve of my departure.

But there is no way to sleep off the memory
of what is forgotten. Only the lemon morning,
bringing eggs and coffee, can rewind the clock.
Only the pink, shaved face. Only the white suit,
the Panama. But memory's gulls are gone.
That great wild rising!
My suitcase, my old Saratoga, are waiting.
Something should have been done.
Once upon a time, something that was not done
still waits in disappointment. *Amor fati!*
Ah, sleep, ah, dreams! *Adieu!*

PART SIX

AN ANTIQUARY OF THE FUTURE

We have nothing like it, dating, I should say, from the mid-Twenty-first Century. Look at those hairdos. The clothes. They just don't make them like that anymore. Here, shake it. It won't break. It can't go away anymore. It is all told. But you see, they still have a touch of the old moonglow? And look at those sunbelt tans. Notice that when you shake it, no snow drifts, only it glows with a kind of sunlight and there are white puffs of cloud in that light blue background. Clearly, it was a beautiful day. But it rained later, see, and the sky turned dark blue, and then nearly black, so that you can hardly see the lovers, and, when it lightens again, time after time, they are different, older and sadder, but kinder. Then shake it again, and there they are again, full of young lust, full of hormones and mean selfhood of the worst sort. It's sad. Dates back to the ancients, the primitives. What's it worth? You can't put a price on a dream like this. It's a classic.

AMERICAN MOBILE

The pure products of America go crazy . . .
—William Carlos Williams

Miss Smith, she dead.

. . . my blind left eye don't stop me
I swivel quick around then get ahead
back at the panorama
striped down and then back up the hill
to any future peak greened brown black cut through
white striped like up the leg on a uniform
the wind don't wall me
my aerodynamics
they'd lift my license for my eye full of sugar
but I still drink
that VA doctor's lower'n fish shit
no beer no way
but I drink Lite test my blood take my insulin
I eat right mostly but my Drake's cakes
I'm thirty-three feet back
sixty-six long times to here
always dreamed of motorhoming
free to be you and me
Maxine's you
she sips at that beer
stares through the wraparound
like she's watching home movies
and shoots bytes at me like look there
did you see that
she's frightened at being sixty next week

I told her look at me—you plus six
and I'm still steering
still truckin' but I never was a trucker
was a kid a soldier a vet a cop and
a guard at Disney's that was my whole damned life
that back there behind me on the road
but it comes along with me in my sugar-eye
my shotup shoulder from War Two
my skin cancer from standing all those years in the sun
reflecting off tarmac and parked cars at Disney World

Max says look Jersey plates
she says Joisey we started out in Jersey
we fell in love haven't slept together in years
Max thinks I'm not well interested
but it's the sugar
I don't tell nobody not even her not especially her
suppose she knew I couldn't
what kind of man would she think
look she says back in back her mother sees it too
I don't know what it is must be on my blind side
but I don't say no way I let them know
I'm blind as a blackboard over there
not hurtling along at eighty
they'd piss their beer
you got to hold to your lane
the old lady's nearly ninety but full of it
not only beer either if you know
look Max says
shut up Max but I don't say it
I don't listen about Alabama moons
Georgia peaches glorious Asheville leaves

I talk to myself my only friend
they suck me in like black holes
the old lady and Max everything goes
into them nothing out toward me
did I believe in love
I've stopped laughing even
I've been driving too long

I see us off the edge of a cliff if I don't keep him awake
old man hunched up at the wheel was he my hero
I think there's something wrong with his eyes now
the way he jerks around to see   I've noticed
I ride not swiveled in a bucket by a tilted instrument pod
but sometimes behind him astraddle his first Harley
his long blond hair snapping in my eyes no helmets
my fingers feeling in the deep holes
through his shoulder and his ribs
where the sniper's bullet drilled through
he died he said and came alive again on a table in
    England
I still wore his white dress shirt
hanging out over my rolled-up blue jeans
shiny pennies in my loafers
Frank Sinatra made me scream Elvis my one daughter
Buddy's blonde princess the Dead my grandson
nobody sings anymore all back there somewhere
with my mother boozed up at ninety
a Depression-made cheapskate
sipping cheap port
and a hundred thousand in the bank
how did we get here

where are we going   why must I come
Harry could save me
clever with life how left-handed he
mangled his right hand in the leather machine
made them think he was right-handed
more compensation
at last a little house and money in the bank
and I got us out of Jersey
like war in the project then
the Sixties the long hot summers
bullets through the windows
down to Max and Buddy in Orlando to my little house
Harry why must I travel with them
the youngsters even are old but Harry's gone
crazy at the end
fighting in the trenches again
Argonne Belleau Wood
gone on the road behind us
dead and buried in Orlando
buried and lost his grave lost
we are going to sue
I have no place to put flowers
no place to talk to him anymore
they lost my Harry
tough leather guy from Brooklyn
tough guy so sweet once
poor old crazy man
gone back to the trenches back to Pershing
mustardgas and Belleau Wood
another world so far away
to his grave at ninety-five
I don't want cable

only my one soap-opera station
only my wine
don't even want life to come back
what is the wind
Star stories say some of us are aliens
supermarket tabloids Maxine calls them
and tries to make me think they print lies
sometimes I think Buddy and maybe even Maxine too
I bore her but maybe pod people have taken over her
    body
like that old movie
maybe she isn't Maxine at all she doesn't act like
Maxine
I could have a baby too
like the hundred year old woman in Australia
it would kill me at ninety they must eat something
yogurt like those Russians who live forever aliens too
and the little girl no older than smaller than
who had quadruplets by a tom cat
all of them born with whiskers
the pictures were right there I saw them
whiskers and pointed ears and long tails I saw them
what is that going by where are they taking me

"Good Housekeeping" said
the kitchen was the warm womb
of the colonial home and early-American women
would stand at the hearth watching the turkey turn
as they pumped up the flames
packing sandwiches for an airline ain't exactly
the big time but we made it
Buddy and I paid off the American dream

for his bedroom and my bedroom
and the alligators down on the lawn
to the rock seawall wanting sun
what's life
put the rocks back put
back build up fall put back
two slices Wonder Bread
one slice waterpumped ham mayo mustard
my long thin fingers all little silver scars
I'm nobody what did I deserve
not Buddy and my mother anyway
sixty ain't the end yet
not even with all my loose belly skin and
stupid strokefoot dragging when I'm tired
like Buddy on Omaha Beach
but I got it right through the head
like being brain-shot and nine weeks in the hospital
stealing our money
there she is sipping her wine at ninety
defying nature and three out of five of us kids with
    strokes
always demanding maybe she gave us the strokes
but nobody's dead yet they say we are all lucky
so that's what luck is not being dead
a case could be made

driving into the dusk is like driving into a dream
better hit the lights
that big cluster of stars down there
I aim my good eye on ahead
now in the dusk it gets tricky
but I don't let Max know

extreme macular degeneration
sugar-induced doc says
then he says you got varicose veins in your eye
laser beams he says burn 'em out
so I see blue for a week from the dye
and the blue fades to gray and that's it
my credit's good
social security veteran's pension Disney retirement
I'm a triple dipper
plus equity in the house poor boy makes good
I'm driving fifty thousand dollars across America
like I started out with anything but
a piano-teaching widowed mother
like I had a chance in life
I play my own tapes me at the organ
singing Willy Nelson songs
"On the Road Again" Max hates my music
she's jealous but says I could of made a living
at it could of but couldn't take the joints
composed some myself guitar piano organ
my tape plays "King of the Road"
my plates say NO MORTGAGE NO BOSS
NO JOB NO WORRIES I'M RETIRED
twenty years standing in the sun eating Twinkies
skin cancer
Harry thought Max could do better
he never had a home like ours right on the gators' water
he'd say he never had alligators on his lawn either
only stinkbugs in his old palm tree
sometimes I miss fighting with him
him on the Kaiser me on Hitler
who was worse all ancient history

even the Commies are dead
nothing left for Freedom to fight
and the world moves moves into the next century
away from us what we did and needed
it'll all be computers and new people
no more like us we're dinosaurs
old people but we move
and we take our houses with us like hermit crabs
we circle Asheville in leaves we land at Normandy
not ten minutes in and all my bones break
until I wake up on the table in England
purple heart silver star
I remember the sea swashing puffs of smoke
our flag it still stands yesterday's news who cares
Max is sarcastic once she was proud
I can't help it Max
it's the sugar sugar

. . . who betrayed me so many times with his Harley
with somebody else's legs around him
fingers in his wounds
hot stuff and joins the police
to wear his beautiful blue uniform
and ride his police cycle with his blond hair
fluffed all around his blue visored hat
and me pregnant alone
with his blonde love in my stomach
stud making a fool of his wife making a fool of his life
with nogood burgling cops only Orlando left for us
thank the chief who saved us and that was when I began
when I began I began began to be old

Maxine looks like me at sixty
you could compare her to a picture of me then
O Harry do you remember
where are we
North Carolina
why are we here climbing this mountain
full of beautiful leaves
is that heaven up there what is that up there
a jetstream
a flying saucer
why don't we just stay home
where I know where things are
they don't think about me how I can't see
how I wish Harry were here
how he was when he was young
so neat courtly so kind and sweet
not like at the end afraid of the Hun
hiding under the table gone crazy old man
with old-timers disease
it was all there again for him
no time had happened
no me no all that life all wiped out
and he was there again and it made me wonder
if we aren't all just here or there or where are we

Asheville we pack it in at Nashville
Max and the old lady won't go to the Grand Ole Opry
so I'll leave them to themselves
I'll go like I always said I would
could hear it in Jersey when I was a kid
could hear it all over the country
Hank Williams Minnie Pearl Tex Ritter

Hillbilly Heaven
a southern yankee I
never get enough of that wonderful stuff
Max says we should of gone the other route
to Memphis first Graceland Elvis can wait I say
but it turns out to be Hank Williams Junior and
  Rockabilly
not like I dreamed of it glitz and bang
even a vet can yearn for the old sweetstuff
Junior's daddy the original Hank the real thing
the lyrics were in a language I could understand
we fought the wars and longed for love
they march for peace and seem to hate
like I'm still waiting for the fat lady to sing
President Truman even introduced Kate Smith
  to the Queen as
"America" *Oh beautiful for spacious skies*
but the Opry's like the rest of it now
maybe we should try Dollyland at Pigeon Forge
no Max wouldn't like it because

angels come to our door but Buddy won't let them in
do you know these are the last days
not if you have something spiritual
it's on Earth
he was sent by the God of Love
that's why Graceland is a church
even if it's like they say
that his body ate twenty Big Macs a day
his soul had to live on Earth didn't it had to eat
so Buddy's blonde daughter tells me
my daughter too but more his blonde like him

now nearly bald not her him not dark like me
well gray but if Elvis could bring happiness
then he is a god

he's one of those aliens Max
he was sent here to sing and bring love
they say Graceland is more beautiful than Heaven
that it's all blue like the sky with no clouds
no thunderbooms and tin-roof rain clatter
where are we

like when Buddy grinds his choppers
he is eating us up in his sleep
our night war like our day war cannibal
shoved our beds apart into separate rooms
trumpets saxophones trombones
Buddy names my snoring while he grinds on
and her crazy on the convertible back there
all night coughs and chatters in her sleep
about chicken wing prices
it's like a gone-nuts orchestra
OOMPA OOMPA CLICKETY-CLICK BLAH BLAH
his teeth telling how much he hates his life
at different times broken uppers and lowers
life that never did what he wanted it to do
we rocked that motorpark in Nashville
hooked up Winnebago nearly laughed itself free
electric lines tore out as it rolled over on its side
and later shaking with screaming
Mama and I had sucked the city of any last drop
of Southern Comfort   Buddy never came back
from the Opry till it was dying out

drunk himself from shit-kicking with urban cowboys
I told him his sugar'll kill him he sleeps grinding his life
like steak into hamburger I'm his life
what's life
Mama refuses to die until we do
gray and stroked and sugared and beer'd under
but how could we leave her at home who'd watch her
nobody'll take her in if we go she has to go
won't go to nursing home no way you know no how
and I don't mean not to go go go before I die
thank GOD for Winnebagos
next stopover next postcard
P.S. life's a war and you can't give up
love Max at sixty

heaven is a place like Graceland
they say Elvis's daughter owns it now
she's the spitting image spitting image
listen Max at least the foreigners don't own Graceland
like they do everything else
it ain't true that we don't work as hard as the Japs
but the unions Max I never did trust the unions

you think like a scab-cop
my father was a union man Buddy

her father was a union man
Harry was always a good union man
and a good Democrat

if they're good for anything the aliens'll be UNION
if I didn't belong to a union

do you think they'd of paid me so much
for making lousy sandwiches
did you get enough sleep
we should of gone to Graceland first
read a "Reader's Digest" article once
first it was the farmlife held us to place
then industry mills and trading and
later the big factories up north
made cities centers now no more
anyone anywhere now the computers
no more fixed life no more unions no more
democrats no more stay put go go go
like the damned beatniks hippies used to do
on the road in the sky
a whole corporation inside your portable
computer workforce anywhere
regions don't mean nothing cities countries
my country 'tis of thee
I'm caught between the old lady back there
and my grandson
he'll be part of it the brave new world he said
college boy and his kids won't even know
what we were
can't you just see it grandpa
no boundaries no borders
even space the moon Mars
business everywhere signals flying through the air
caught between times becoming part of it
losing it at the same time
with my sugar walking down the street
I never noticed how sweet beer is
injections they'll be able to fix that too grandpa

and the whole world and even space
will become AMERICA

you look at your mother and you think
how could I have come out of that sixty years ago
HAPPY BIRTHDAY Max
it's a chorus of whiskey-cracked voices
a duo of dead and gone ghosts
calling back over their shoulders
it's bye-bye Maxine you're as good as dead
with your mastectomied pumped-up plastic tits
what'd you need them for for *him*
could of caused the stroke I'm told
but then why my brother and sister stroked out too
my face I had burned with acid and scraped
for him forty years ago
acne pits from her tea and cheap day-old cake
to stuff us just before supper all of us
faces like burned-red moons
from her brother-can-you-spare-a-dime
cheap Depression soul
the old man back from Belleau Wood
mustard gas and the formaldehyde stink of the tannery
the whole goddamned century's been a war
I could live to see the end of it
no more goddamned Twentieth Century
now we fight each other we can't stop fighting
we're like three hairy-assed Marines
landing on each other's beaches
HAPPY BIRTHDAY Maxine
Christ he kissed me breath like death blow out my
  candle

if I could I'd blow them out of the Winnebago
and get my wish a little time on earth alone a little life
before I die

Max was always tough even as a little girl
she always fought
her father'd have to drag her off
from a fight but he was proud
my Max don't take no shit he said

we had to be tough Jersey we all glow in the dark
better than hard cold and cheap
we had nothin' but trouble like the plague
Nineteen-Nineteen she says
the doughboys brought the influenza back from Europe
all those displaced persons
my best girlfriend died of it everybody
was dying you're too young to know
good to be too young for some things
why do you think God does it
screw that
God helps them who help themselves Buddy
he likes that one   damned Republican
but he's right it's like Elvis
a success a blond guy with black hair and a cape
God loves us all Max He's sending them to help us
well He's got a damned funny way of showing it
your granddaughter says He sent Elvis
or is it Elvis sent her
I told her he came in on a saucer
they'll all be here soon

Buddy singing playing the organ he installed
coming in on a wing and a prayer
his feet pumping he loves to show off
he says Harry was just a leather worker
says my mother taught piano   class will tell
your people don't have no class no way
then it's a Donnybrook
in the musical world

in heaven this couldn't of happened
if Max would spell me
I'd go back and get drunk with the old lady
sit in my *Seat w/Telescoping Pedestal*
and stare at her until I could see inside her BRAIN
but Max won't spell me won't drive no way no how
just sucks in sixpacks and farts at speed bumps
I'm mustard gassed like Harry at Belleau Wood
turn on the BTU's she says watch out
open the vents here comes Max
but she admits it was damned embarrassing
we got the Arizona state troopers all over us
here's the old lady telling the pump jockey
at our time of life we want full service telling him
I'M BEING KIDNAPPED BY ALIENS
I have a lovely home in Orlando
they're forcing me to go with them
they want my money a hundred thousand dollars
it belongs to Harry he earned it with the wrong hand
call the police help help
it takes some explaining but I tell them I'm an ex-cop
look I say but they got me and Max over a car hood
if I had one of those BIG FOOT trucks

I'd drive right over top of this traffic jam
crushing cars like an angry giant
that's why everybody loves Big Foot
I look at the cops and twirl
my finger in a circle at my temple
nuts the both of them I say
they feel sorry for me and because I'm an ex-cop

get real Buddy do you think God's in California
or in the Painted Desert or the Petrified Forest
I want to see the first Disney place is all
Max is *mad* like Mel great roadman
people say it's the end of America
from the coast there on it's out forever
and the sea climbs into the sky
Buddy it's your music
sometimes you sound like some godawful poet
song of the open road Max
there's good trucker songs Max
trucker poets cowboy poets
you're ignorant Max
don't start Buddy don't start
I tell you what Buddy
Vegas is God
you get a bucketful of change and pull handles
until something good happens
gangsters built Vegas Max
gangsters built everything Buddy
Bugsy Siegel is God and Vegas is heaven
for shame Maxine
what do you know Mama
it's all a chance and to hell with your aliens

can't you see saucers Maxine
clouds Mama we're in the mountains
Sierra Nevadas Mama
I'm not *your* mother I'm hers maybe
and the white bombs of love
like the Star says it's Elvis in his saucer
lots of Elvises because this is the end of time
they have big dark eyes and sideburns down to here
real smooth cheeks and they wear wonderful jumpsuits
with colors like Las Vegas that night
the first or second so it was stacks of colors
and everything blinking they wear clothes like that
with glittery things hanging down from their sleeves
I was a little girl when Dreamland burned down
my mother your grandmother Maxine
said you could see Dreamland burning from Jersey
I had been to Coney Island I had been to Dreamland
I'm sure I saw Vesuvius erupt and a great naval battle
where New York was bombarded by foreign ships
and then an American admiral went out
and defeated all of them
you see children it is all a dream
and you keep waking up to something new
we aren't really here at all we are here
and somewhere else at the same time in Dreamland
Meet me tonight in Dreamland under the silvery moon
my mother used to play that one Mama
I am not your mother don't call me Mama
you're alone in the world Harry never liked you
motorcycle-head he called you
Maxine's got me if she is Maxine
of course I'm Maxine

Christ of course white bombs
SNOW
where are we Maxine
if I smashed this pedal down down hill
I saw a movie once about a wagon train full of people
heading west on Donner tha's it the Donner party
they were going over these very mountains
they were up here
high like this and there was a blizzard
and they got caught
and they couldn't get down out of it
blizzard starved and they began to eat each other
don't look at me Buddy
the saucers will save us
they'll snatch us up into Graceland
they can do anything they can make us fly
can they take us back to where they came from
is it a musical place
of course it's a musical place
Elvis is King
yeah Graceland is the real true blue heaven
beyond the cheap chicken wings of the world Mama
beyond the world Maxine
or whoever you are
Buddy my ears just popped
we're climbing Max
it's getting dark Buddy
you better stop
can't stop on the highway
some articulated eighteenwheeler
some BIG FOOT
come behind us

no visibility
now I nail my one good eye
to the white-dark wraparound
like one big cataract
faint red lights
turning off ahead
now nothing
down there's a turn
somewhere down there
I hit the gas down hard to the floor
it's dark and white like being wrapped in ermine
if we weren't doing eighty ninety a hundred
it's like a toboggan like the OLYMPICS
SWOOSH SWOOSH and we're out off in SPACE
the cold moon and stars ahead
I push my *WING-EXTENDER* BUTTON
and now it's STAR TREK
THE PANORAMA OF SPACE
I can see through the thick clusters of stars
ahead there deep
GOD'S BRIGHT MUSICAL CASTLE
but the saucers hold us floating in air
HIGH OVER GRACELAND
you can see the lights
I told them I told them
and THOUSANDS and THOUSANDS
of GOLDEN COINS COME GLITTERING
CRASHING OUT

HERACLITUS

for Elbert Harkins

I. POSTCARD

You are growing old, & too sad for your own good, judging
by your last missive where you wrote that you were tired

of reading bad unrhyming *vers libre*, as you put it,
& newspaper headlines filled with murder & mayhem,

& that we humans are merely the slaves of all we survey,
meaning I take it the slaves of our impulses & not

the lords & owners of our faces as Shakespeare wrote
in one of those sonnets of his which you used to read

as others read the Bible, the Bible which you attribute to lesser poets
whose muse is a God in whom you do not believe.

Is it your loss of my proximity that has led you to this depression?
For you seem depressed & lonely, & I'm sorry I had to move away.

I had a family to care for & this distant spot served the purpose,

& now one child has a child & there are others here on
   the way.

See the photograph of the lake on the other side of this
   card—
it is beautiful here, but let me tell you something about
   it.

Out on the lake fishing the husband of the woman next
   door
was stung by a bee & died before he could dock.

He was a slave to the lake & the fish, I suppose,
if you are correct when you say we are slaves to all we
   survey.

The bee must have been a slave to the man in the boat
since he got close enough to lose his stinger to him.

But I am also writing with reference to unrhyming
   Kilroy
whom you deplore & who has just won the Nobel Prize.

Actually Kilroy writes both with rhyme and without
as did Shakespeare & Whitman ("O Captain! My
   Captain!") & Frost.

Even now I am writing you an unrhyming poem called
   "To a Sad Friend."
Why not come & visit me—we can go out & fish on the
   lake.

The fish & the bees can survey us & be our bright
  slaves
& I'll do my best to cheer you up about Kilroy

& meaningless unrhyming poems & mayhem & murder.
You can look at the children & see there is some good in
  life.

II. ROANOKE RETURN

Now, six-hundred miles above my southern exposure
my friend in extremis waits,
a man old enough to be my father,
and I am heading up North Carolina
in the long heartless dark,
to big, bad, only-the-dead-know Brooklyn,
headlights blazing on high beams,
being blinked at, warned and horned
—for I am faring to where one half
of my split spirit dies, in my war hero
drinking buddy, Elbert, two silver stars,
two purple hearts, smiling up ahead of me,
wan smile of age: Normandy's gone.

Tarheeled, tarwheeled, I wend my way,
blinking lights streaming into my brain,
to Brooklyn, that Elbert calls God's,
over hills of North Carolina night,
knowing the running greens and pines along the road,
how they set themselves against the running moon,
in my camouflaged combat jumpsuit

big enough for Santa jumping Claus,
soaked through with unholdable brew,
while the moon swings . . . the two moons
. . . and Elbert swings . . . in and out . . .
of the Fort Hamilton Veteran's Hospital
with his lungs smoked away, brave as ever—
Elbert, I give you a new medal,
the moon, the two moons, one for each
black lung—we will jag together once again
in your unbelieved-in-God's country,
where you might be looking at the moon, too.

It is a mad quest of hope and love
up 77 to Roanoke, link up with 85,
smooth overdrive to Harrisburg,
up the night to Jersey, climbing up,
up the great flying sky-harp cathedral Verrazano
and dumped at your Fort Hamilton feet—
Elbert, I salute you!

My olive-drab seabag bounces in back
like a wild love pregnant with burning vodka
and cheap-at-the-source Carolina cigs, deadly
gifts Elbert begged me to bring, only sooner,
in time for us to enjoy them together,
a lifetime of death brought now
and become magic to stop him from dying,
burning and unburnt offerings!
. . . in and out of smoking clouds,
lightnings, with the moon in and out,
escaping, seeking, avoiding love, age,
death, my wife, children, responsibilities

that begin in dreams . . . waves of water,
wind pressing me across lane lines,
and I am in the fast lane, pulling
around a slow-climbing eighteen-wheeler
honking like a tug, beaming me down,
wet speed and mild madness streaming away behind me.
It is a hot shower in a Roanoke motel room
and a nightmaring, dream-drunken sleep.
It is black coffee and a long-distance call,
and it is all too late, for me, for Elbert,
Officialdom now in charge of his skinny bones
—I hoped the metastasizing crab broke its teeth
on the embedded shrapnel that for fifty years
stabbed out through his skin in bloody stigmata
—and it is the long sad hungover journey home
in a day dark as night and relentless rain
falling down Virginia, North Carolina,
it is "Pardon me, boy . . ."
on the static-stuttering radio,
blanking, blanking out in the low country,
and it is the wrong rainy road, ascending . . .
looking out at water-colored what?
A Wailing Wall of water—
and I am high and outside, low and inside,
denim-backed white-duck fog and no lights, no cars,
no world but rain, alone, blood-shot eyes cotton-blind,
gearing up and down, burning brakes, clutch,
going round the side of something big
—the wet rockface of a Great Smoky,
with the steaming abyss of eternity below.
Elbert the Brave, be here as I quake,
strengthen me, breathless, on high,

going down, down down down too fast,
I dip, I spin, I slide, I am sideways,
backwards, tottering at a precipice
facing the past, rocking, rocking, stopped.
I am in heaven with nothing but down on one side,
hungover, scared—ALIVE—with the land down under
wet blue and green between layers of stranding smoke,
money in fog banks, and I pull off, away
from one possible end, sidestepping death.
All praise to Elbert, I am steady.
Love, I will be home tonight!

CONTRA MORTEM

— a suite

I. THE ROSES

The wishes live together in unease.
I see no stasis, but a perilous balance.
I watch as roses disassemble, petal
and petal, touched with darkened tips
and edges, and think of when they bloomed,
how determined their becoming,
how absolute. I have watched the gardens.
I have watched them carefully and long.

I think the wishes live together in unease.
Just when the turn comes, I'm not sure.
The roses hold and hold late in the year
but at some point surrender, at some point

you can't identify, it seems before you see it,
and you are looking, looking long and hard,
and then you realize that it has happened—
the roses wither, fall.

It's true that the wishes live together in unease:
the thing you knew was magic—you look again—
is just pedestrian. Is it because
you know more than you did, or have you lost
a knowledge you possessed? The wishes live
like twins who hate each other, jealous twins,
who want your only love. Live, says one, Die,
the other; and they stare across
your holy land like enemies, but finally
they compromise, and hold the ground they have.
And this can last most of a lifetime, like
the freshness of the rose that holds throughout
most of the summer and almost into winter.

II. THE NURSING HOME

There are more women than
men in the nursing home and
more men than old doctors.

Staff doctors visit once a
month. The few old men do
very little but sleep. Two

or three of them occasionally
gather outside in clear
weather for a smoke, which

is allowed them. I suppose
those in charge feel that
it can make no difference

now, and it brings the old
men a little pleasure. I
sit and chat with them

sometimes. Perhaps "chat"
is a bit too lively a word
to describe what passes for

conversation during these
puffing sessions. A lot
of low grunting goes on.

There is one old man who
is afflicted with bone
cancer and who says, in

high good humor, that his
guarantees have run out.
He was a travelling salesman

in women's wear, and still
remembers how much he loved
women. Many of the women

have become little girls
again. They carry dolls
about with them, mostly

rag-dolls, I suppose so
they can't injure themselves
when they squeeze them.

To see these toothless,
balding old ladies, frail
as twigs, clutching these dolls,

is heartbreaking. Oh, to love
something! It's still there.
It has been in them since

they were little and had dirty
knees and bows in their hair.
Some recognize me now, and,

when I give them a wave,
they wave back. It's a
wonderful feeling to make

contact, but it is difficult
to tell how much they know.
The care-givers are kind and

efficient. They are mostly
young, and apparently try
to imbue the old with some of

their zest for life, but
of course the old know all
that already—or knew and have

forgotten it. I wonder,
can the young reverse their
situations with the old

and see themselves looking up
at such fresh faces from the
vantage of bed or wheelchair

or walker? I am too young
to join the old here in the
nursing home, this metaphor

(or is it the tenor of a
metaphor?) for the last days,
but I am too old

to feel the buoyancy of the
young; so, at least for the
context of the nursing home,

I have arrived at yet another
awkward age. After visiting
my mother, who is only partly

present, I go out and sit
with the old men and have a
smoke. We hope for clear days.

III. WHERE ARE YOU?

What life does to us
is strange, too strange,
I suppose, for many to
think about. But I
think about it, about
how you were here,
right here with the
rest of us, and now
are not, are gone into
the ground and maybe
are waving in the grass,
or are sitting silent
there, being the rock,
or are looming up
and reaching out,
being the tree, or are
drifting easily down
the street, being
the leaves burning
and the smoke.

Where are you?
You cannot not be anywhere.
I want you to come back;
but you can't, I know.
I can fan the air
with my hands and
do no good. I was
sitting here, right here,
with you, and you were

saying or doing something
and I was not attending,
I was thinking my own
thoughts, but what
are they now? I
should have listened
deeply to you. I
should have recorded
your voice in my mind,
so that I could hear you
again and again until
I myself am smoke.

IV. LOOKING DOWN AT A FRIEND

for Patrick, R.I.P.

Always, now, truth is the tight suit that you wear.
You twirl your diamonded cane as you dance in
    stillness.
Forever takes you no time at all, so you can't
be expected to wait for those who loved you, slow
alive and grieving unlike your fast asleep self
playing on the moon, transported everywhere at once.
Friend, you seem not to miss your old friends, you
seem to be busy elsewhere, unfaithful seeker.

Dare you not remember those who loved you? Dare
    you?
Whom you have caused such suffering? What do you
    seek,
now, in the no-wind wind, in the no-place place

where nothing is most powerfully itself?
Lying there, where are you going with your stolen self?
You were always one on a journey somewhere, even
when still.

V. NEWS OF 45

Into his mid-life crisis
desperate man stalks wild
life brings home head of
thought for wall display
mounting it for worship
plenty yet more to come
proudly shows it to friends
who scoff saying some
body else got it for you
like hell they did shot
gun see all the holes
in it but its mine mine
mine proud of it autumnal
macho laughable necessary
joy so worry not thy heart
days of glory upon thy
wrinkled brow sparks
of plenty more to come
next better yet which
could be worse who
knows but plunge on
plunge on with no effort
for light takes you
smilingly home as you

stay & practice your
declensions sun-o
moon-a your conju
gations selvesyes
selvesalways selves
before selvesafter
glory glory glory
for my five & forty.

VI. HEART FAILURE

I have made my moon landing at night
by way of the emergency ward,
on the strong black arm of a nurse.
My wife is the other woman,
and between the two women I enter,
seeing, reflected in glass, my red car
half up on a curb, and mal-angled,
the glare of the high beams showing
my terrified wife's confusion.

There is no air in that car,
there is no air in the night,
but there is air in the hose that the nurse
claps to my turning-blue face,
and strength in her arms that are used to
the harsh struggles that have plagued her existence,
strength that I finally can share in.

I lie in a gown in a room,
and the silent killer says nothing.

He signalled, I guess, with red flags.
I paid no attention. I'd developed
an elephant's hide, an armor for the arrows
of insult that poor boys endure.
From childhood, when I was raw,
and my nerves could actually bleed,
I worked on this suit of armor,
oiled it and flexed it and shined it,
but now it belonged to them,
the doctors who probed me with wonder.
"Didn't you notice a thing?
You sound like a sidewinder, rattling."
"I thought I'd caught cold in the chest."
But I had no desire to know
because I had no desire to stop.
I could see that they thought, "What a fool!"
All but the black nurse, who knew
how the poor slid the slippery slope
that poverty, stress, and high blood pressure
grade for the struggling-upward.
She pulled at my ear, and said, "Tough guy!
He don't take no crap from his heart."
She knew how the pressure builds up,
as you climb in the ignorant ghetto,
until you would break, or be broken.

"How you doing, baby doll? Better?"
"Yes, but now I'm embarrassed."
—embarrassed at being so weak,
ashamed of my heart that can fail,
ashamed to have such a heart—
no lionheart, no Coreleone, I.

But they tell me it's stress that's at fault:
the heart is okay, the tests show.
The angel nurse flattens my hair,
pulls at my ear, and says, "Go!—"

VII. HOUDINI AND THE DYING SWAN

Where was he? Was it a tunnel?
But he had come to a wall,
a slimy, wormy wall.
He must break through.
He must break out.
He felt for a tool.

Naked, she lay back in the tub,
white as a white swan, long-necked
as a swan, thin as a silken thread,
her gloriously thick dark hair
piled loosely up, collapsing
onto her wide, sloping shoulders,
dark, water-dipped ringlets forming,
her swan's-down skin pinking,
steam misting her swan song,
her suicide with water and razor.

ii

They concentrated. A glittering
company. Rich. Celebrated.
They waited for the great Houdini.

His monument was dark, unmoving.
The stars glittered, like the company.
Half a minute. They breathed
in short, shuddering breaths,
and waited. Houdini heard:
"Houdini, do not disappoint us,
for we must believe that Death
cannot take us, utterly."

Tearing at the wall, his long
yellow fingernails cracked off,
ricocheted; then he heard:
"I am dying, dying . . ." He drew back,
prepared to throw his body at the wall
—he must *break through . . .*

iii

The steaming water in the marble tub
was streaked in ribbons of red.
She was going to die, that *he* would know,
her lover, what he had done.
He had killed beauty
in neglect and pursuit of money.
He would be sorry. Her long lashes locked.
It was like a dream, and she was falling,
falling over a dark sea, which now she struck.
The noise jolted her. It was like
breaking plaster, like tumbling bricks,
like an earthquake. Her eyelids rolled back
to see a mad-eyed specter

emerge from a great, gaping hole
torn through tiles. Her dizzy mind,
half-bloodless, saw the bloodless form,
and fainted. Houdini lifted her from
the marble tub and taped her wrists.
He put her in her bed and tugged
the bell pull. She was too beautiful to die.
A great grandfather clock obliterated
the last of midnight. A doorknob turned,
and he went back the way that he had come.

Houdini darkened into death.

VIII. DEATH

What do I know about death?
It is a question one must
occasionally ask oneself
Death who are you what are you
No metaphor will do
because that is merely
a likening of one thing
to another thing, which
when it comes to death
is impossible, for
death being unknown
anything we should
choose would be
arbitrarily chosen
and therefore
would be a bad

metaphor nobody
being able to say
how close or distant
the vehicle
from the tenor
the subject being
death. How then
do we approach this
unsubject this
antisubject this
but you see
even here
is a metaphor
even here
we are at a loss
that we are asking
a question for which
the only answer
is death.

IX. LEADBELLY

for the musical ghost of Blind Lemon Jefferson

Leadbelly, grim with your Cajun accordion,
with your harmonica blues, with your knife
   flicking down the twelve strings of your guitar
—*the Rock Island Line was a mighty good road*—
bowing, scraping, white-suited trainman . . .
made your pride sick, but you sang,
   fast, strong, quiet, like a driven
demon, like you had to get it out

    before a razor dumped your guts
on a blood-mud taphouse floor,
    or some drunk crazy rednecks
nailed you up like Christ, in a dangerous world
    for anybody but most America for a black
poet of low-down places and sky-high loves.

    Leadbelly, thirty years hard time murder,
six and a half, sang your way out, ten more, intent,
    then Alan Lomax and his bro, John, folklorists—
makes you laugh inside at night—white boys,
    playing—but they get you out again and in
the Library of Congress, that grinding
    voice part now of something big, like
storm darkness, like that lifething,
    love, always beyond somewhere or
crying deep inside, in a dark place,
    yeah, big like music, big like that gal you
call Irene! How many Irenes, you think?

    Even the Lomax bros, even them white boys,
they know Irene—you driving them through
    New York traffic, them folkloring in back and you
being their folkloring black chauffeur.
    You drink sharp liquor in Harlem, play
with Woody Guthrie, Sonny Terry, Brownie
    McGhee, the Headline Singers—radio too,
Hollywood and *Three Songs by Leadbelly*,
    a French tour . . . . You show 'em your razor
stretch marks, your shotpitted pot.
    Good night Irene I'll see you in my dreams . . .
all that good hot mean hard American life

and Lou Gehrig's *amyotrophic lateral sclerosis*.
It's *The Midnight Special*!   Fade me, Death!

X. ANTHOLOGIES ARE SAD

Impressed by smoking-ember music,
as I have always been, drinking gin,
and reading the poets of the past—
who are in anachronistic pain
as if alive, striving, thriving
today—I think of today's.

I have a new anthology,
one including me,
with, alas, dates.
Most have only births and dashes,
a few the flying ashes,
the smoking music, of the past—
dates that say, *At last! At last!*

What then of Berryman
and those other merry men
and women who were human—
in pain and joy—alive?
In the anthologies they thrive,
possessing their due dates!

So now I turn a page,
afraid to find my final age;
and, though my last is but a dash,
I feel the flutter of ash.

XI. BECAUSE

in the port-cities they have found everything out and
Aristotle-like have put everything into categories
and the unicorn is an ungulate because they say so
because the fine-print of the unreligious sun says we
    circle it
it is not for us but we for it because the moon hit us
and bounced off instead of was born of our first spin
because the ninth planet is an invading comet caught
and because there is no now and there never has been

because we look upon ourselves in savannas past
knuckling to water because we see the white lemming's
    hole
in the snow smashed down by hooves and hear its
    pitiful
chirp of counter-aggression because the avalanche
indifferently buries the contested world of the snow
valley because stars die because we believe in facts
and because the deluge led to the ark because because
and because we bury our dead and dig up their bones

because the unsoundness of our judgments lead to
    sound
judgment and because facts are facts and we must
    reckon
and because the sea is cruel and because time flies
because the wind blows down our houses and because
we remember the snow hare and the hawk because
because the dove is taken in air by the eagle
and because space is either empty or full of dark matter

because galaxies hold for a long time their pinwheel
  shapes

because time and space are curved and we can blow
  ourselves up
and because we blow ourselves up constantly and
  because
it makes us wonder because doesn't it mean something
because we are riding a mud-ball through space because
we were born here and because we have categories and
because we dig up our bones and dogs dig our bones up
and because we are not even safe in pyramids because
we dig ourselves up and look upon our own bones

XII. A HUNDRED YEARS

Although the sea won't pose,
the picture that the boardwalk takes is clear.
In each ear, the old man says, he has a baby mouse
that squeals sometimes and makes the surf high-pitched.
A hundred years of being here, he says,
seems merely like a day, a day with many nights.
Once, he kept the old lighthouse, once, a tackle shop,
and once he was a fisherman himself, also selectman
  once,
but then he laughs and says he married twice.
Most of the Earth, he says, is sea,
most of a man is water,
and mother comes from mare and meer and others,
the sea we swim before our birth.
Once, too, he was a farmer,

and calved the cows inland, but not for long.
The sea must call him back, he must have the sea,
or the sea have him.
In a hundred years you learn a thing or two,
he says, but not so much as you might think.
Mostly it's the magic of it all.
You are born with that, you have that right away,
but then there's sex, and then there's all
that business in between that's meant to keep us going,
the race I mean, and you forget the magic
in the business, the busyness, he adds,
and you work hard, and you are tired a lot, and only see
    the sea,
as with your mind and not that sense the youngest have
that's gained again in age, when time's more free,
and you can feel the flow of life right on your skin.
You feel the wind, now, I don't doubt, but do you feel
the other thing? Do you feel the secret thing?
Do you feel the thing behind the wind?
Aldebaran was so bright last night,
I 'most could take it in my hand,
not so simple as a jewel, but a spiritual thing.
When I look at the sea, or at the stars at night,
I do not fear my hundred years as you might think.
They do not wish to go or stay.
They are always here with you and everything.

I am always happy to drop everything—pretty nearly—when I make the acquaintance of a new poet as good as E.M. Schorb.
—James Dickey

E.M. Schorb's "The Journey" navigates among dreams, déjà vu, premonitions, a carefully observed, scrupulously interrogated present and "a touch of the old moonglow." Sometimes, he even seems to bring dispatches from "the undiscover'd country," but he is always rooted in the world of the senses and the mind. It is a pleasure to travel with him.
—R. T. Smith

The poems of E.M. Schorb shine calmly even as they buzz with energy; are connaissant with the world and yet transcendent of it; make something deeply funny and yet highly sad—given a world and a time and a good mind's eye. This is the work of a mature intelligence, its ironies unadulterated by cynicism, and its swells informed by understatement
—Heather McHugh

E.M. Schorb's poems do for me what great poetry should do—they illuminate experience from inside out, in poetry that shimmers with luminosity. Welcome to the "Hotel Paradiso" where "The Journey" begins.

—Sander Zulauf

"The Ideologues" is a profoundly bitter indictment of those writers who prostitute their art to support fanatical revolutionary politics. Schorb demonstrates a versatility in free verse that matches his proven ability as a formal poet.

—Joseph S. Salemi

"The Journey" will take you deep into your mind and soul. You'll ask "where does the sun come from," you'll try to "discover the source of pain" and you'll "rejoin yourself, deserted long ago." E.M. Schorb has discovered the 'Higgs boson' of the poetic world, the vision that binds it all.

—Pat Mullan

To be a first-class poet requires a fluency of language, mastery of a vocabulary sufficient to express seminal, original thoughts set down with rhythm, with imagery, and with descriptive evocation that communicates flawlessly with the recipient of the poetry of verse. Such is the case with the poetry of E.M. Schorb.

—*The Midwest Book Review*

www.ingramcontent.com/pod-product-compliance
Lightning Source LLC
Chambersburg PA
CBHW021827090426
42811CB00032B/2060/J